Letters to Bowen

A Time Capsule

Alice Lachman

Order this book online at www.trafford.com
or email orders@trafford.com

Most Trafford titles are also available at major online book retailers.

Printed in the United States of America.

ISBN: 978-1-4269-5488-7

Library of Congress Control Number: 2011905814

Trafford rev. 11/21/2011

www.trafford.com

North America & international
toll-free: 1 888 232 4444 (USA & Canada)
phone: 250 383 6864 x fax: 812 355 4082

LETTERS TO BOWEN

LETTERS TO BOWEN

A Time Capsule

Alice Lachman

Trafford Publishing; Bloomington, Indiana

FOR BOWEN

ACKNOWLEDGEMENTS

My deepest gratitude is due the following for their help in putting these little "stories" into book form:

Sarah Tullo for giving me the idea for this book with her "time capsule" request, and for always being there for me. She is a great daughter, wife, and mommy who gives her all.

Kent Tullo for his technical help, for countless helpful suggestions, for his loving support. Most importantly, for being a funny, loving, wonderful daddy.

Peggy Grimes for proof reading, editorial suggestions; but most especially for many years of friendship and support.

Matt Hartman for his memories, his patience with my computer difficulties, for cheering me on day after day.

Jane Tullo for all she is to our beloved grandson, and for allowing the telling of some of her adventures with Bowen in his book.

Evelyn Lachman for allowing the telling of some of her stories. Thanks especially for being there for my children as faithfully as if she were their grandmother. As in every other area of life, I have learned from her.

James Hartman for contributing his memories and allowing some of his stories to be included. For gently allowing compromise when neither one of us nor our children could recall the exact details of certain events. We all agree, however, that the spirit of the stories remains intact and true.

Linda Joy Sands for allowing her story to be told in this volume, and for her wholehearted ongoing support over the years.

Marigold (JoAnne) Klemmer for her poem "A Beginning." Thanks as well for her precious friendship and continuing support, distance notwithstanding.

Alice Lachman

<u>Karen Passons and Ed Samples</u> for permission to use their names and for their part in Maggie's story. Beyond the thanks I can express in words, my heart is so grateful for their allowing me to adopt Maggie, the sweetest little black dog anyone can imagine. More than just a dog, she is my faithful companion, my good example, my precious little friend. I know her transformation from a broken street dog to a regal lady is largely due to the love they both gave her. Ten thousand thanks, Karen and Ed.

<u>Catherine Cifelli</u> for her long ago yet still relevant advice to "put pen to paper." Her words have driven me back to the computer more often than I care to admit.

<u>Karen Peterlin</u>: for her generosity in proof reading this manuscript. Her corrections, given with honesty and integrity, have been invaluable. I am grateful as well for her friendship and encouragement over the years.

INTRODUCTION

When my grandson Bowen was one year old his family gathered to celebrate at Grandma Janer's house. It was a wonderful party. All of us were glad we had been invited. We were happy to celebrate the first year anniversary of this little boy.

The invitations sent by his parents specified "no gifts" since Bowen had so many toys, clothes, etc. Sarah, his mother, asked instead for a gift for his "time capsule". I had no idea what that meant. Sarah was not helpful in answering my questions about gift giving for the child. She just told me something would come to me. Alas, nothing did.

Weeks later, she and I were having a conversation at her house, and she asked me how we celebrated birthdays when she was a little girl. I gladly told her about her coming to me the very first thing in the morning of each birthday, to sit on my lap and hear the story of the day she was born. This was before anything else could happen on her special day. I would tell her about Aunt Evelyn coming to take care of her brother Matthew, the trip to the hospital, how wonderful the nurses were, how her daddy was there, how long we had waited for her, and how happy we were to finally meet her. We would have her Uncle Tav, Aunt Evelyn, and others come to share cake later in the day, while her brother would be the "giver" of all the birthday gifts. He would decide which gift to give based on what was in the package if he knew, or based on his curiosity if he did not. On his birthday their roles were reversed. After hearing this tale Sarah exclaimed gleefully, "Mom, I just love your stories!" That remark answered my question about the "time capsule". I decided to write some stories for Bowen. Most of these stories are about happenings in my life, in my children's lives, my grandchildren's lives, the evolution of my belief system, and other memories joyful and sad. Although the book was written for my grandson Bowen, I would like to offer it to others. I encourage those who choose to read this book to write or record their lives in some way for their own progeny.

Although now, at the age of three, Bowen cannot read this book nor understand much of it, eventually he will be able to do just that. I hope then if I am still alive, he will read it to me. If not, then I will have left a legacy which I hope will comfort and inform him when he wonders about who Grandmom was, and what it was like in the "old days."

TABLE OF CONTENTS

THE BEGINNING

Dear Bowen,

For your first birthday your Mommy requested that guests at your party gift you with items for a time capsule. You may know by now about time capsules. They are meant to be reminders of things past. I think they are good things. The most important thing about them, in my opinion, is the vision they give to the very young about the lives of those who are older.

Sometimes time capsules are put into or under buildings, or in the cornerstones of buildings. Items in the capsules might tell about the building itself, or perhaps the past use of the land. Maybe there was a different building in that place which was removed to make room for a bigger, grander building. There is always a difference of opinion about these things. You will have to make up your mind as you grow. Was this a good place to put an office building? Or was it a good place for a hospital? Or a little cape cod house like the one you came home to when you were born.

I decided for your birthday time capsule I would begin to write some stories for you. Some of the stories are true. Some are about events in my life. Some are about your Mommy's life. Some are about you. Some are about people I have never met, but whose stories touched me in some way, deep in my heart. Some are dreams I have had. Dreams sometimes inspire so I would like to share some of my dreams that have made my life richer than it had been before my dreaming. Some are about events or ideas that came from deep in my heart. Probably the reason I thought to write about these things which I feel so strongly is that my love for you, your Mommy, your Daddy is so rich, powerful, and deep for me.

I will start with a simple story. I remember when your Mommy told me you were going to be born. I was very excited to hear such good news. At the time we did not know if you would be a girl baby or a boy baby. We just knew we would love you; in fact, we loved you already although we had not yet met you. A long time went by before you were ready to be born. Then one night your Mommy called me and told me you were almost ready. All night I tried to sleep so I would be rested and so be able to encourage your Mommy and Daddy to do the work they would have to do for your birthday. I was much too excited to sleep. In the morning your Mommy called again to tell me she was going to the hospital where most babies are born these days.

I went to the hospital to meet your Mommy and Daddy. They too had been very excited and had slept little.

They thought you would come soon. But you took your time, and by the next night we were all still waiting for you and we were very tired. Your Mommy was the most tired. Your Daddy was next. But probably you were the most tired of all. Still, we waited. We loved you so much; we were so eager to see you. We knew then that you were a little boy. We knew your name would be Bowen. How we loved you!

One thing that touched me deeply during that time was the way your Mommy and Daddy worked together to birth you. Of course your Mommy did the most physical work, but your Daddy was so caring and tender with her. He showed so clearly his love for her and for you. When the midwife suggested your Mommy shower and let the hot water run over her back she did not think she would be able to get herself into the shower. Her labor was making her very tired. So your Daddy said, "I will go into the shower room and help you". He held the showerhead and put the hot water on your Mommy's back to help her relax. He washed your Mommy's hair and combed it to help refresh her. It brings tears to my eyes just thinking about it. I cried then too, seeing how hard your Mommy worked for you. You are so loved.

Finally you were born and the first persons to hold you were your Daddy and your Mommy. Later I was able to hold you too, and the moment will live forever in my heart. You were such a beautiful baby, and your life was all before you. I tried to send good energy to you so you would feel loved always; so the way through your life would be supported always by great love. No one has an easy life, but for you I wished the hard times would never break you, but rather temper your strength; make you courageous, stalwart, and dedicated to your good dreams.

This is all for now. This short story is one of the true ones in this little gift for you. I will try to write often. None of us has enough time to do all the good we wish to do in our lives. For you, I will try to record some of the times most meaningful for me. Perhaps they will have some meaning for you too.

With much love,
Grandmom

Mommy, Daddy, and Bowen
"Homecoming"

DANCING WITH MY GRANDMOM

Dear Bowen,

This is the second story from me to you for your time capsule book. It is about a dream.

In my dreams I have some special friends who come to me. They sometimes accompany me on my dream adventures. In dreams things are not always as they are in awake time. In this dream my friend Hawk came. She was quite large in this dream. You see, in my dreams Hawk and her friends can alter their size and they can talk to me. In addition, sometimes my dreams are "waking" dreams, as this one was. That means I am awake while dreaming, but not totally awake. I am less aware of events around me than when I am fully awake. Sometimes these dreams are called "daydreams."

Teachers tend to not like it when children daydream in class, and they sometimes give the message that daydreams are not good. In fact, although they can be distracting to the student and the teacher, they are actually very important, very good. You will learn more about this as you grow. Now, back to my dream....

I was in a rain forest. The trees and undergrowth were very thick and it was hard to walk. I had a machete, however, I did not want to cut any of the plants to make a path. I worried that cutting them would hurt them. I did not want to inflict pain or injury on this important vegetation.

Hawk suggested she fly across the forest with me on her back. This we did for some time. I liked being able to see the forest from above. But the canopy (the top of the trees, very thick in these forests) was so dense Hawk was having a hard time getting through. Suddenly we saw an elephant on the floor of the forest. She trumpeted (that is a loud noise made by elephants, often a greeting) to us and suggested we land on her back. This we did. Since she was so big and strong she was able to walk through the thick growth without much trouble.

Elephant walked quite a long way through the forest and we were singing as we went along. I was thinking about what a nice journey this was; I wondered where it would end. Of course the journey is always more important than the destination. Suddenly I saw a figure on the ground waving to us. Imagine my surprise when I realized it was my Grandmom!

5

An aside here is to tell you who that is for me. I am your Grandmom because I am your Mother's mother. Your Father's Mother is also your Grandmother, but she uses a different name for herself with her grandchildren. She is your Grandma Janer. So my Grandmom in this dream was my Mother's mother. I called her "Grandmom", as you call me, and as my children (your Mommy and your Uncle Matt) called my Mother. Enough about background now, on with the dream.

The last time I saw my Grandmom she was old and sick. It was not long before she died. Everyone dies of course, but we continue to live in the spirit world, which is where we come from in the first place. In my dream she looked just the way she did when I was a little girl. I lived with her then; she took care of me. In my dream she was laughing (how I loved her laugh), waving, and calling out to us. We were on Elephant, as you surely remember.

Elephant stopped, picked up my Grandmom with her trunk and gently placed her on Elephant's back with us. Grandmom was excited to see me, as I was to see her. My Grandmom was so important to me growing up, and she is still important, much loved by me now. Grandmom pointed to where she wanted to go, so Elephant took us a long way through the forest. After some time we came to a little clearing. Grandmom jumped down from Elephant and began to dance. She called to me to hurry up so we both danced in the clearing. I cautioned her to avoid exerting herself too much, as I remembered her as old and sick. She laughed and said, "I look old, but I am young inside!" She meant that in the spirit world, where she lives now, she is young and strong, but she looked to me as I remembered her when I was a little girl. This was so I would recognize her in my dream.

We danced for a long time in that clearing until I woke up. It was one of the nicest dreams I can remember because I had not seen my Grandmom for a long time. I do think of her often. Seeing her in my dream was wonderful. Dancing with her was awesome!

I hope you dance often, Bowen. Also, I hope you have dreams that cause you to wake up to music with love in your heart and a big smile on your face.

With much love,
Grandmom

This is a picture of my Grandmom, just as I remember seeing her in my dream.
Although she never met you, I know she loves you, as she loves all her children,
grandchildren, great grandchildren, and her great great grandchildren.
You are one of her great great grandchildren.

MOMMY, UNCLE TAV, and COOKIES

Dear Bowen,

Today I was thinking of you when I went to Friendly's with a friend. There were balloons there and I remembered how well you said "balloon" last week when you, your Mommy, your Daddy, and I went for lunch at Friendly's near your house. There were balloons there too. You pointed to them and very nicely told me they were balloons. I was very proud of you.

This reminded me of something your Mommy said when she was only a little older than you are now. We often used to visit my brother Tav. He lived near us and we loved to visit him and his wife Evelyn. My brother's real name was Gustav. His daddy's name was the same except his daddy was called Gus. Calling both father and son by the same name could become confusing, so instead of giving my brother the nickname "Gus", everyone started calling him Tav. I liked the name, and Tav eventually got used to it.

Your Mommy called him Uncle Tav. When we went to visit Tav, he often went to the kitchen and asked your Mommy to accompany him. She liked going with him. He would ask if she would like a cookie and she would say yes. She could not say "cookie", but would say "tookie" instead. This amused Tav who thought your Mommy was the cutest nicest little girl in the world at that time.

One day she took a cookie from Tav and went into the living room to eat it. She was smiling and happy. She remembered to say "thank you" to Uncle Tav. We had a dog who would never take food from your mommy. The dog's name was Gypsy. Although she would never take food from your Mommy, she would take food which was on the floor. She thought it was there for her.

On this occasion your Mommy suddenly started crying. Tav went running to see what had happened to her. She was upset and empty handed. She told Uncle Tav, "I dropped my tookie on the thor". Of course as soon as the cookie hit the floor Gypsy ate it, lickity split. That means very quickly. Tav was so touched by your Mommy's tears he almost cried. He picked up your Mommy and took her back to the kitchen. He dried those tears and gave your Mommy another cookie. Can you tell he loved your Mommy? She loved him too, and they still love each other.

There is one other little part of the story. Some time later Tav called me to come to the kitchen. He told me he was very upset with your Mommy. "Why, I inquired?" He answered, "She just asked me for a cookie!" I understood. Tav liked to hear your Mommy say "tookie" but she was too grown up for that now. She had learned to say "cookie". It seemed a little like the end of an era, and he was a little sad to know he would not hear her say "tookie" any more. But at the same time he was proud of her because she was learning to speak like a big girl.

Of course I thought of this event when I saw the balloons in Friendly's and I remembered how nicely you are able to say "balloon". We are all very proud of you Bowen. If you say "cookie" right away that would be fine. If you say "tookie" for a little while we would like that too. Know that your Great Uncle Tav loves you and is proud of you no matter how you say and / or like your dessert. This is a true story about your Mommy when she was a little girl. Ask her if she remembers.

With much love,
Grandmom

Formerly a "tookie", now a "cookie".

UNCLE MATT TO THE RESCUE

Dear Bowen,

Today I was thinking about stories for you. I thought of one about your Uncle Matt. He likes to write his name with the "@" symbol, which means "at". If he writes M@ it is rather like his name; he uses that symbol a lot. When you learn to spell this will have more meaning for you.

One time when Uncle Matt was a little boy, about three years old, his Daddy and I went with both our children (Uncle Matt and your Mommy) to visit a place where they were building time share resort condominiums. Your Mommy was about two years old then, just as you are now. We climbed a big hill to where a snow lift was being built. It was very pretty there with many trees in the hills. Uncle Matt wandered into a little clearing and was playing happily as toddlers tend to do.

Suddenly Uncle Matt called out to his Daddy and me that there was a dog crying nearby. Neither his Daddy nor I could hear a dog. But Uncle Matt persisted and his Daddy and I walked over to where he was in the field and there his Daddy (your Grandpa) heard it. Then I heard it too. The cries were rather pitiful. It sounded like a very little dog, perhaps a puppy. Uncle Matt led us to it. He followed the sounds of the doggie cries and there she was. She was indeed a puppy, quite small, and she was crying. She had been abandoned there on the side of this little mountain. She was wet, cold, frightened. She was wet because it had rained the night before; it was autumn so the night was cold. The day was chilly too. She must have been frightened because she was left there alone. She was so cold she was shivering so I put her under my shirt to help her get warm. There she quickly fell asleep. Soon she was warm and dry. Still, she slept.

When we got home we decided to keep her although we had two other large dogs. I thought she would be a little dog because she was so small when we found her. When she was fully grown she weighed about 75 pounds, which is not considered a little dog. Oops! I was wrong about how big she would be. But I was right that she would be a very good loyal companion. Soon after we decided to keep her I took her to our vet who discovered she had been outside for a considerable amount of time. She was sick. He gave her medicine to make her well. Soon she was happily playing with the other dogs. We tried to think of a good name for her. Since she was black and white, rather roly poly as a puppy, your Grandpa thought she looked a little like a panda bear. The name was perfect for her.

Here is another interesting thing about Panda Bear. She was raised in the woods where we lived when Uncle

Matt and your Mommy were little children. Panda Bear learned to come when she was called. She learned to sit and wait at the door but not run out or knock people over in her eagerness to get outside to play. She never learned to heel because she did not need to know that while living in the woods. Later, when she was about 11 years old we moved to a town so she needed to know how to "heel." Just as most dogs do, she liked to chase squirrels. Therefore, when I walked her on the leash and told her to heel she did not understand that I wanted her to walk beside me and not run ahead or chase anything. She kept trying to run and I held the leash and repeatedly said "heel." She looked into my face to see if she could figure out my odd behavior. After a few days as we were again walking and not understanding each other, Panda Bear suddenly stopped and looked at me. If dogs can smile she was smiling. She got it! She never again needed a leash; she knew what to do. When I said "heel" she walked beside me and did not run until I told her it was OK for her to do that, usually when we were away from the street and it was safe for her to run.

This turned out to be two little stories in one bigger story. One little story was about Panda Bear; the other was about your Uncle Matt and how he felt sorry for the puppy and wanted to help her. We did help her. She turned out to be a help to us too, by caring about us, trying to protect us and keep us safe. That is what Ozzie is doing when he barks at people who come to the door or walk too close to your house. The people who come to your house are not a danger, but Ozzie is just a dog who cannot read so he does not know that. He just tries to protect his "pack" which includes you, your Mommy, and your Daddy. It includes me too when I am at your house. I am so happy to be part of Ozzie's pack because that means I am part of your family. What a good thing that is for me!

With much love,
Grandmom

11

Here is Uncle Matt pretending to give you your first "driving lesson."
When he was a little boy his Daddy, your Grandpa, used to let him "drive" just like this.

The black dog is Panda Bear. She looks a bit like Maggie, but she was much bigger.
Panda Bear weighed about 75 pounds, Maggie is smaller at 55 pounds.
The grey dog, Panda Bear's friend, is Fred.
The human in the picture is your Grandmom, many years ago.

AUNT EVELYN

Dear Bowen,

You have met your great Aunt Evelyn on at least one occasion, and she has often spoken of you since then. Aunt Evelyn is my brother's widow. That means she and my brother were married for a long time before your great Uncle Tav died in 1993. If my math is right they were together for more than 37 years. Evelyn has not married again. She is the matriarch of her line. That means she is the oldest living woman in her family. She has two sons, one daughter, one grandson, and one great granddaughter. Her love and pride in her children is beautiful to see.

There are many stories I could tell you about Aunt Evelyn. All of them show how caring she is about others, especially her family. She is my sister-in-law but since I never had a sister I think of her more as my sister. She is your great Aunt, your Mommy's Aunt, my brother's beloved wife. I now know I have several half sisters and brothers. However, I have always known Evelyn as family.

The first story I remember about your Aunt Evelyn is that she and your Uncle Tav met in high school. They went to the same church and continued in that church all their lives. While in high school Tav made rings for them of stainless steel in shop class for them to wear. They were a kind of engagement ring. Later, they married and wore gold wedding rings.

They lived at first in a little house in Glenside, a part of Reading, Pennsylvania. I used to visit them there. This is one of my favorite stories about Evelyn. She was cooking dinner for her family. I said I would help. She asked me to use the mixer to mash potatoes. I tried. I had never used a mixer before, so I did not know I needed to keep the beater straight up and down in the bowl. In case you are not aware of the consequence of letting the beaters move from that position, I will tell you. Potatoes flew all over the table, walls, sink, floor, everywhere. Evelyn did not yell at me, regardless of the mess. She just asked me if I had ever used a mixer before. I admitted I had not. I should have told her that in the first place. Oops. Needless to say, she taught me to use a mixer, so I never made that mistake again. She taught me lots of things, often just by her good example.

Many years later, my Mother died. That is a story for another time, but I will tell you part of it now. I went to the hospital to say goodbye to my Mother, who was in intensive care. Your Uncle Tav and your Mommy went with me. We had all been up all night and we were very tired. After Mother died, your Uncle Tav, your

Mommy and I went to a nearby diner for coffee. I ordered home fried potatoes since they are made very differently in Berks County than in New England where I live. Of course I preferred the Pennsylvania style. When the server brought the potatoes they were the same as those served in New England. We laughed at that. As soon as we got back to Tav and Evelyn's house my brother whispered into his wife's ear, "My sister has a yen for home fries". Evelyn did not say a word, but she got out the potatoes and started peeling them for our breakfast; she was making eggs with toast at the same time. I had been crying because my mother had just died, but I was so touched by Evelyn's caring and concern about my yen for "real" home fries I started crying all over again. Then we laughed. Evelyn has a wonderful sense of humor and a great laugh.

My mother died as a result of a car crash, so her car had been towed to a repair station. The car was totally destroyed by the accident. In order for the car to be recycled the "title" had to be signed over to the person who would be sending it for recycling. A few days later Tav was on his way out the door to take the title to the repair station when I noticed he was leaving. I asked him where he was going but he did not give me a direct answer. Evelyn correctly guessed where he was going, and said she would go instead. I protested, saying I would go. None of us wanted to look at the car in which Mother had been so badly injured. How do you think we resolved this impasse? Right, we all went together. It was hard to see the car but we hugged each other and got through it, each of us supporting the other. This is the sort of thing we learned from Aunt Evelyn. She was "Great" Aunt Evelyn in many ways.

Aunt Evelyn is retired now, but she still works almost every day. She takes care of little children. She loves the toddlers because at their age, that is your age, they are interested in everything. They are very curious. She reads to them (you like to have books read to you), she gives them snacks (we all like snacks), she helps them put their toys away, and helps them put their coats on to go home. She loves those little children almost as if they were her own. May we all show our love by caring for each other as your Aunt Evelyn has always done. That, more than anything else, is what makes a family.

With much love,
Grandmom

15

This is a picture from your baby shower, held in your honor shortly before you were born.
Although she is not in this picture, your Grandma Janer
was the central planner for this wonderful party.
From left to right: Uncle Matt, Aunt Evelyn, Joy, Mommy, Grandmom, Jill,
Grandma Sue, Grandpa, and Nana.

GRANDMOM'S BIRTHDAY DRUMS

Dear Bowen,

Tomorrow I will be coming to Clover Street in Milford, to your house to visit you, your Mommy, and your Daddy. I love my visits to your house, although usually they are too short. This visit, however, will not be too short. This visit is a little gift to myself for my birthday, which will be next Wednesday, November 13th. I was born in 1941, which as you can imagine, was a long time ago. Even your Mommy and your Daddy think it was a long time ago. I must admit that is true. Next Wednesday I will have lived on this planet for 66 years.

One thing I would like to have for my birthday is a Remo Djembe drum. These are made in the United States, using pvc plastic material for the body of the drum and synthetic material for the drum head. It has a nice sound and is light, so it is easy to carry from place to place. This particular Remo drum has a nice pattern on it; gold stars and moons on a purple background. I think you will like it. Of course just being with family and friends is the best thing about birthdays and holidays, even without any gifts at all.

The other thing I wish for is an African drum. I thought originally of getting another Djembe from Africa, but I found a slightly different drum called a Bugaraboo. It is similar to the Djembe, but the top half of the "hour glass" shape is longer than the Djembe, making the sound considerably deeper. I bought the drum as a birthday gift to myself. When you come to visit for Thanksgiving I will show you my new drum so you can play it with your own little hands. I cannot wait to hear the nice sound it will make.

I decided to give my new drum a name. I will call it "Uhuru" which is the Kiswahili word for "freedom." I have always liked that word; I especially like the meaning. Kiswahili is the language of the Swahili people who live in East Africa. My Bugaraboo drum was made in Mali, a rather poor country in West Africa. The capital is Bamako, which means "Hippopotamus" in Bamara, the local language. Most people there speak Bamara, although the official language of Mali is French. One of the most interesting things I know about Mali is this. There are no large supermarkets there, nor stores for clothes or furniture. Rather, there are open markets on the streets where people sell their wares, including drums.

The most recent additions to my drum collection are from the "Heartwood Project." This organization provides education for poor children and teaches job skills in addition to language and mathematics. One of the skills the children learn at the school is the making of drums and drum bags. Those who are very poor or live far from the school can live at the school until they are graduated and have a job so they can earn their own living. I have three drums from the Heartwood Project now. They are without question beautiful to the eye, the ear, and the heart. Now you can see when people grow up they can buy things for themselves. They need to be sensible about it, but not always totally practical.

Thank you for bringing such big smiles to my face, Bowen. You are a great gift from the divine to me, to your Mommy, your Daddy and all the rest of your family. Here is a different ending for this (true) story from your Grandmom. I WILL SEE YOU TOMORROW!

With much love,
Grandmom

Here you and your Daddy are playing my new Bugaraboo drum.
The "ropes" on the drum are used to tune
the drum by tightening its head.

<u>SHOPPING AT HOME; CIRCA 1940s</u>

Dear Bowen,

Today there are shopping malls everywhere. Some are in large buildings; some are in smaller buildings in a row near a street. These are called "strip malls" because they are built in a row, or a strip. These days most people shop in malls. One of the reasons I like where I live now is because I do not often have to go to a mall. There are some malls in the area, but there are many stores in the downtown as well, as there were when I was a little girl. My mother loved to shop, and she would often walk downtown (four blocks south and eight blocks west) to shop in the "downtown" where the stores were located. When she had made her purchases she would walk home. I often went with her, but it was a very big walk for me when I was little; I was always quite tired when I got home. I seldom walk far now to go to the stores. This is partly because I do not particularly like to shop, and partly because the distance is considerably more than twelve blocks each way. Still, it pleases me to see the people on the sidewalks going about their errands. It also pleases me to see all the other activity in town.

In Northampton, a nearby town, there is much to do and see. I have gone there to concerts, to dinner, to plays, to shop, and just to watch the people walking about. It is a rare treat these days to see a vibrant, busy, thriving downtown anywhere. Having this in my own backyard is wonderful. Soon you and your Mommy and Daddy are coming to visit and celebrate Thanksgiving. We will have some time to sit and chat, lots of time to cook turkey and eat, but not that much time (this time) to see the sights. We may have a chance to go see Mount Tom, my favorite hiking place in Massachusetts. Mount Tom, some people say, is the highest mountain in Massachusetts, which is not saying much since mountains here are considered hills elsewhere. The Andes and the Alps and other mountain ranges are very high, but our little Mount Tom at least has the distinction of being big in a little place.

But I digress. I was talking about shopping. When I was a little girl I did go downtown with my mother, but I liked the home shopping the best. Now I shop quite a bit online, and it is a bit like shopping at home. But when I was a child the shop came to me. We did not have television or internet then, although we did have a telephone with a party line, and we had a radio. Instead of the internet we had merchants who came with milk, ice, vegetables, (called produce) and bread. The thing I loved most about these merchants was that they produced the products they brought for us to buy. The milk was brought by the farmer whose cows gave the milk. The vegetables were brought by the farmer who planted and harvested them. The bread was brought by the baker who baked it. The ice was cut from a large outdoor area deliberately flooded in the winter by the man on the wagon. It was kept in a cool underground bunker called an icehouse, covered with sawdust, until he brought it to us. I will tell you more about ice later.

The best part was that the people who brought the food carried it to us on a wagon, pulled by a horse. The horse was always beautiful to me. I remember one horse was a lovely caramel colored brown. She often stood on three legs when she was waiting to move on. The horse was not lame, rather, she just rested that way. The horse would let the "resting" leg touch the ground with the tip of the hoof, with no weight on that leg. Some time when you go for a ride and see horses in a field look to see if any of them are standing like that. I have seen them stand on three legs often, in fields, at horse shows, and of course on my street when I was a little girl. Another really great thing was the horse knew the route the farmer would take and she would stop and start with no one driving the wagon. The farmer would take items off the wagon and go from house to house selling it, or people would come out of their houses to pick their choice of produce off the wagon. As the people on one end of the block had their deliveries or had chosen their goods from the wagon, the farmer would whistle a certain way and the horse would start walking. Later, the farmer would whistle again and the horse would stop. I thought at the time that horse was as smart as anything.

There is one more thing. Do you remember I mentioned ice earlier in this letter? At my grandmother's house, where I lived for the happiest years of my childhood, we had an ice box. Most people these days have never heard of an ice box. I loved it, and I sincerely grieved for it when we were finally able to get a refrigerator. Here is what the ice box was like. It had three sections, one on top of the other. In the middle was a large insulated door with the kind of latch one sometimes sees in the meat section of large food stores. Of course those refrigerators are much bigger than our ice box. It was cold in there and we kept milk and leftovers and other perishable food in that section. Above it was another large section with a big block of ice in it. The ice served to keep the food in the middle section cold. It worked a little like a lunch box or cooler you might find at a picnic with ice in it to keep food or beverages cold. The ice was not sufficient to keep frozen food frozen, so we could not keep ice cream or frozen foods in the ice box. We had to eat those foods quickly since we could not keep them frozen. The bottom section (you remember the ice box had three sections) was smaller and very close to the floor. The deep tray in that section slowly filled with water as the ice block melted. The water ran down the sides of the ice box and collected in the bottom tray. My Grandmother emptied it every day. On rare occasions she would forget. When she came downstairs in the morning there was water all over the floor.

As you now know, the ice box did not have electricity or other means to stay cold without the ice in the top section. Because the ice melted it was necessary to buy ice every few days. Thus the man who had cut those large (about 18 inch cubes) blocks of ice would bring ice to our house. He had large tongs with sharp points and big handles with which he would grasp the ice and carry it into the house. We had a sign which he provided; it said ICE in big letters which he could see from the street. If we needed ice on the day he was scheduled to come to our street we would put the sign in our front window and he would come with the block of ice so our food would stay cold.

This is a true story of a different kind of shopping at home, without using computers or telephones. It is a happy memory for me because it was part of the place which felt like a safe home for me. There is one more little detail. When it was hot in the summer, my Grandmom would offer me a cold treat. She would open the top part of the ice box and chip a little piece of ice from the big block and let me eat it. I loved doing that, partly because the ice was cold and refreshing, and partly because having my Grandmom chip the ice and give it to me made me feel special and loved.

You are loved too, Bowen. You certainly are special to your Mommy, Daddy, Grandparents, including me, as well as to all the rest of your family. Enjoy your shopping trips, and sometimes remember with me about the horses and the ice man.

With much love,
Grandmom

Here is a picture of a brown horse such as that which brought food and ice to our house when I was a little girl. Notice it is resting its left rear leg. (This horse has a white mane similar to your Grandmom.)
Dreamtime photograph used with permission.

GRANDMOM'S WALK IN THE WOODS

Dear Bowen,

When I was about seven years old I took a walk in the woods. It turned out to have much meaning in my life all these years later. But I am ahead of my story.

I used to spend summers at my Aunt Ruth's house. She was my Mother's aunt, my Grandmother's sister, making her my great aunt. I called her Aunt Ruth. She lived in the country, on a truck farm. No, farmers do not grow trucks on truck farms. Is that silly or what? Truck farms are small farms where vegetables and sometimes flowers are grown. Aunt Ruth had several acres at an earlier time, but she had sold some land to a neighbor. Since she did not drive a tractor nor even a car, she could neither plow, nor cultivate too many acres. Still, she kept enough land to grow lots of vegetables and flowers.

The neighbor came to plow for her early each spring, but she did all the rest. She planted, weeded, cultivated, and harvested all by hand and all by herself. She planted all of her two acres and when I was there she let me help a little. She let me weed in the flower bed and without knowing what the flowers looked like compared to the weeds, one time I pulled up lots of flowers. Aunt Ruth was upset, but not angry. She knew I did not do it deliberately so she just tried to teach me what the weeds looked like. I still have some trouble with that, but since I am not often called upon to weed anything which I have not planted myself, I can usually remember what to avoid pulling up. After my mistake at Aunt Ruth's I would stop and ask her if I was not positively sure of any plant being a weed or a flower.

Every kid who visited was allowed to catch Japanese Beetles and put them in a jar to give them to Aunt Ruth. It seemed a little odd to give these to her, as if they were a gift. But it did prove to be a gift of sorts since the beetles ate the crops. Catching them and putting them in a jar saved some of the vegetables she grew. I remember the beetles had little pinch parts on their feet so they could climb over the plants, under leaves upside down without falling off. I felt those pincers on my fingers as I caught the beetles; I was amazed at the wonder of the detail and adaptation of those little creatures. They were pretty too, with iridescent colors and wing covers which protected their wings as they crawled on the plants and ate, then opened wide just seconds before the wings spread when they took flight. I felt special since I was not only able to catch beetles, I got to stay there at Aunt Ruth's house overnight. In fact, I lived there most of the time in summer when there was no school.

Aunt Ruth's house was at one time a two room school house. It was heated by a little coal stove in the living room and a big coal stove in the kitchen. The cooking was done on the kitchen stove and I really liked knowing how it worked. It had several round circular parts on the top of the stove with grooves in them. There was a special tool which fit into the grooves and allowed the lifting of the circular parts without the need to touch them; they were very hot. The coal was put into the stove through those holes, and ashes were removed via a small door in the front of the stove. There were tiny shovels to do that work. Sometimes I would bring a small pail of coal in from the coal shed.

There was a bathroom in the house with a toilet in it, but it was not hooked up. Aunt Ruth's first husband, Uncle Bill, was going to install the toilet and put a sink in that room, but he died before he finished the job. So we used the outhouse. Do you know what that is? An outhouse is a small structure which looks like a little house, or a shed. Inside it has a kind of primitive seat with a hole in it. Under the structure is a big hole in the ground and when people need to go to the bathroom in the outhouse the waste goes into that big hole. Occasionally the big hole is filled with dirt and the outhouse is moved to another location. That is a rare event.

As you can imagine it is very cold going to the bathroom in an outhouse in the winter so when I was very little I was allowed to use a "chamber pot" at night, at least in winter. It was a ceramic pot with a lid. I remember one night I looked for the chamber pot and it was not there under the bed as it had always been. I asked Aunt Ruth about it and she said I was old enough to use the outhouse regardless of the dark or the cold. I had mixed feelings about that. I was proud to do such a grown up thing, but I surely did miss the chamber pot when it was cold or raining or snowing… But I digress.

There was a little forest behind Aunt Ruth's house but I was not supposed to go there. My Mother was against it, thinking I could get lost. When Mother was not there, Aunt Ruth let me go into the woods because she knew the area was so small I could not get lost for very long. She, like my Grandmom, said she believed kids should be kids. They should do kid stuff. So I went into the woods and I loved it there.

I remember one day when I went into the woods it was early in spring. The trees were growing their new green leaves. I was on a small path, no doubt an animal trail since it was so narrow. Since I was a little girl at the time I had no trouble staying on the path. There in the middle of the path was a tiny green plant just poking its head out of the ground for the very first time. I was very moved (that means a profound emotional response) by seeing it, so I squatted beside it and looked at it for a long time. As I looked I thought about it. How did it know to grow like that? If the seed were placed in the ground upside down would the root grow out of the ground and the leaves grow down? I found out since that no, the roots would still grow down and the leaves up.

I decided that some wonderful being or some benign force must have made it possible for plants to do that. As I looked around I saw so many trees and other plants I was overwhelmed by the majesty and goodness of this creation. I have never forgotten that moment and the feeling I had. It took me a long time to realize that what happened to me there was a spiritual experience, an awakening. Some people spend their entire lives without such a moment. I am so grateful for having had that time, and for being able to remember it so clearly. I can remember the path, the trees, the little plant I saw, the questions which filled my mind, but most importantly, I can remember the feeling I had on that day.

I spent many years after that day, looking for a connection to that which I could not name, but which I now knew existed. I had many adventures along the way; I will tell you more about those at a later time. You may want to save some of those stories until you are a little older, but as you can see, children have an open heart for such stories and you may not want to wait.

One more part of this story, which by the way is true. Before I left the little forest I walked close to a stone fence. The farmers would often take the big stones from the fields and put them at the edge of the field so they would not interfere with the crop growing nor the machinery used to plow and cultivate and harvest. There at the edge of the forest, lying on a stone fence in a sunbeam, was a snake. It was a rattlesnake; I could tell by the sound of its rattle and I could see its markings clearly. The snake looked at me and I looked at it for a long time. I knew it would not come toward me to harm me, and the snake apparently could tell I would not harm it since it make no move to run away, nor did it repeat the short rattle it made when it first saw me.

I loved that snake. It represented nature and the divine for me in a way which few things have done since. May you too see the divine around you every day in true tangible forms which move you deeply.

With much love,
Grandmom

UGA1361253

This is an Eastern Diamond Back Rattlesnake.
Can you see its rattle in the middle of its coil?

This photograph was taken by Jeffrey J. Jackson of the University of Georgia.
It was provided by EDBR Forest 04, Bugwood.org
It is used here with permission.

PHILADELPHIA, PENNSYLVANIA

Dear Bowen,

When I was a little girl I lived in Philadelphia, PA. Incidentally, that is also where I was born. It is a big city, and it has a rich history. Our nation was also born there. Of course our country was first a concept in people's minds. They talked about it, then they met in what is now called Independence Hall in central Philadelphia to sign the Declaration of Independence. That document is considered to be the foundation of our country, a very long time ago, in 1776.

One of the things I remember about living in Philadelphia is the lamp lighters. Your house has electric lights so the wires conducting electricity is the power source for those lights in your home. At my house in Philadelphia we too had electric lights inside but outside on the sidewalks, guess what? No electric lights. The street lights were powered by gas. One of the things about those gas lights is that they had no on/off switch as your electric lights have. You can turn the switch in your house and the lights turn on. The gas lights had no such switch. So how did the lights go on for the street lights? This was such fun for me. A man came on our street every evening carrying a ladder. He probably was pretty strong. Even if it had been an aluminum ladder it would have been quite a burden since he had to go to so many streets to light the street lights. But in the 1940s there was no aluminum. All ladders were made of wood. So the man would come and put the ladder to the lamp post. I could kneel against the back of the couch in the living room and watch the lamp lighter (that is what the man was called) climb up the ladder, open the gas valve, ignite the gas, climb down the ladder, and go on with the ladder to the next lamp post. I could kneel against the back of the couch in the living room and watch the lamp lighter climb up to light two or three lights on our block each night if I timed it right. Sometimes I had to help my mother with some chore and I would miss seeing him, but not often.

Lots of things were made of wood at that time. Many materials which are commonly used now were not available then; some because they were not yet invented (such as plastic) and some because they were rationed (such as rubber and some metals). Rationed meant only a little was available to each person or family. The reason is that 1941 to 1945 are the years when the United States was involved in World War II. Most of the important supplies were given over to the "war effort." Many metals, rubber, and other things fell into that category.

I am thinking of your little stroller. Your mommy and I took you to the park and to the beach in that stroller, and sometimes just for a walk. I remember one time it started to rain when we were "strolling." You did not mind. Your stroller has a kind of hood which keeps you dry if it rains. Your Mommy and I did get a little wet, but we did not mind either. When I was a little girl I had a stroller too, but it did not have rubber wheels as your does; (remember the "war effort"). Those wooden wheels made such a clatter on the sidewalk. Even though it was a long time ago and I was only a little girl, I remember that noise. It was even louder than the trolley cars, which were very loud. The only metal in the stroller was the axel and the hardware to keep the parts together. The entire stroller was made of wood.

Some time when you come to visit I will play some music for you from the 1940s. It is quite different from some contemporary music but we liked it at the time. I like to listen to some of it still. No doubt you too will enjoy many styles of music over the years. So now you know some of what it was like in the 1940s. Perhaps in 2072 you will enjoy writing some of your stories to a wonderful little boy whom you love very much.

With much love,
Grandmom

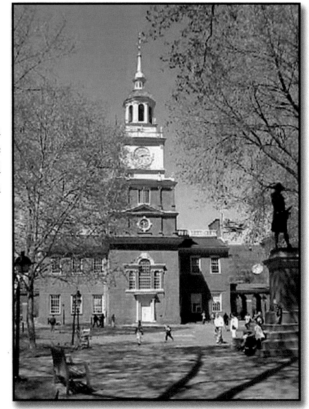

This is a picture of Independence Hall in Philadelphia. Both the Declaration of Independence and the Constitution of the United States were signed there. The Liberty Bell, rung at the signing of each document, is also housed in this building.

This is a picture of my Grandmom, my Mother, Tav (my big brother), and me in the backyard of our house in Philadelphia.

THE "HOLIDAYS"

Dear Bowen,

The holidays are coming. Holidays mean many different things to different people.

For Christians, December 25 is the birthday of Jesus, whom they consider to be the Son of God and the savior of all humankind.

For Muslims, it is the time of the celebration of Ramadan, a time of fasting with a feast and celebration at the end. It too is focused on purification and salvation.

African Americans have lost much of their culture and religious traditions by their enslavement here in the United States. These unfortunate people were not allowed to worship in their own way. They were not allowed to speak their own languages. They were not allowed their music, their culture, nor were they allowed to be with their own families. If they wed and had a child, the child and parents were not allowed to be together, so one was kept and the other two were sold. This continued until the slaves were emancipated. Sadly, the freed slaves had no memory of their homes in Africa, nor their language, nor their customs, not even their religious practices. In recent years, in order to regain some of their lost customs, African Americans have begun to celebrate Kwanza, a gift giving, earth centered belief system which honors those who were enslaved as well as their current tenuous ties to Africa.

For the Jews, there is Chanukah. This commemorates a time when the Hebrew people were oppressed by the Romans. Their ability to hold out under siege was aided by a lamp which burned for eight nights with only one tiny bit of oil. The Jews see divine intervention in that, so they celebrate their special relationship with God by giving gifts and burning one candle in a menorah (nine branched candelabrum) each night for a week and a day.

The oldest tradition we know about is the Pagan celebration of the winter Solstice. Newer religions tied their celebrations to the time of the solstice so the Pagans would embrace those new religions. For Pagans the Solstice was very important. Pagans did not want to take on the new religions. They were happy with their own beliefs. Since the new religions celebrated at the same time and took many of the old ways into their own rituals, eventually a kind of conglomeration evolved. For instance, the Druids and other Pagan groups used to decorate trees outside in the woods to honor the earth spirit, their concept of the divine. They called the trees "one leggeds", a term still used by Pagans and by Native Americans, who have their own belief systems. Those have less to do with the modern religions than some of the other traditions. People who adopted the new religions thought the trees were pretty when decorated and so began cutting them down and incorporating them into their traditions and rituals. Of course the decorating was to honor the trees, to honor nature. Unfortunately, cutting trees down is the antithesis of honoring them. The people did not know that, and the practice persists into today. One important point, the people who decorated the trees put lights on them, first candles, then electric lights. This was to anticipate the hoped for return of light which is marked by the Winter Solstice.

At one time people did not realize the sun was not going away when the hours of daylight diminished. They knew they needed light and warmth to grow the food they needed to live. There was fear, sometimes even panic when the daylight hours were very much shorter in the winter. The cold frightened them too. Nothing much can be grown in the winter in the cold and the dark. So the people prayed and danced and hoped for a "miracle" so the sun would return and sure enough, the sun did just that. The longer hours of daylight and the warmth returned to the earth; the crops grew in the summer as usual. Eventually we learned about astronomy so we understood why the hours of daylight predictably got shorter and then longer without magic.

All the religions above mentioned have had the same roots. Those are from long ago when people feared starving or freezing in the cold and darkness. They worshiped in their panic, ignorance, and fear. Although better educated now, people still celebrate the Solstice and in some ways they even take on the trappings of the Pagans. Jesus is called the "light of the world" in the gospel of St. John and in many other places. The Jews light lamps to bring light into their world as well. The Africans also use candles as do the Muslims and other less well known religious groups. Even the Buddhists and Hindus use candles and incense. The incense is a sign that the prayers being offered are rising to God, who is pictured as being "above" us by many religious groups.

In our family the traditions have been largely Christian, since most of the family, both sides of both sides for many generations have been Christian. This is neither a good thing nor a bad thing in my mind. It is a respectable and honorable choice of faith and tradition. For many years I too had a very strong Christian bent to my thinking and my faith. Let me explain a little about my journey in that department. I was not brought up in a particular religion, although my parents were nominally Lutheran, therefore Christian. I wanted to belong to the Lutheran church because my brother (your great Uncle Tav) sang in the choir in that church. Although I knew nothing about the church or the religion, I wanted to be able to sing with him in the choir. I had to join the church to do that, but first I had to be baptized. Some churches, including Lutherans baptize children when they are babies. For some reason I was not baptized as a baby, nor as a little child. As I said, the family was "nominal" in their relationship with the church. So I was baptized and I joined the church and I sang with my brother. Eventually my image of God evolved, until membership in a particular church seemed unnecessary, even counterproductive. As I studied and pondered I grew to know that god is not far out there, but is deep inside each of us. Inside every being and every part of the universe is a fullness of life and energy. This is the divine presence in my mind. It makes more sense to me than the idea that god is apart and separate from us. Of course that is only my opinion. It explains why the rituals of any one particular tradition are not so important to me. I like many rituals from all traditions and I use them in my own religious practice. It is very interesting to me that so many diverse traditions have the same core, and the same values. For all those groups salvation is a gift from the divine, and cannot be earned nor bought at any price. It is freely given with great love.

So let us get back to our family traditions. We used to have a birthday cake for Jesus on Christmas day. We gave presents to each other as well. That took all day because the youngest in the family was the giver and the others opened their gifts one at a time with the youngest taking turns opening theirs too. It was fun. Sometimes the day was a little lean in the present department but we always had a good time. We also had a tree all decorated with lights and ornaments. You had one in your house last year, although you may not remember it because you were a wee one then. This year you will be able to help with the decorations and giving presents. We have always taken time to be with family as much as possible for the holidays which include New Year's Day as well.

Your Uncle Matt is part of the holiday season. He was born on the day after the first day of the New Year. A big meal is usually consumed by all at this time, similar to Thanksgiving day, but not always turkey. I prefer ham or other meat, coming so close on the heels of Thanksgiving. It does not matter what is on the menu. It matters to be with people we love and it matters that we let them know we love them. Nothing much else is important. Maybe it is because I am older now, but my priorities have shifted significantly with age. I like that. You will too, but you will have to wait a long time for that to become obvious to you. You will see it in your parents first, as they see it in me now.

This is just a little about the "holidays." I know you will have a wonderful time this year and I look forward to seeing you and your tree. Do not be disappointed if there is no tree or no turkey or no ham or no presents. The best Christmas I ever had was one which featured few gifts but instead had lovely music and much caring. There will be more about that at another time.

31

Remember to be true to your own beliefs. Let your self grow in them. Do not be so attached to this or that ritual that you cannot grow to your next stage of development. That is as important in your spiritual life as in your shoe size. I know you understand what a shoe is, and you can even say "shoe". Eventually the rest of the story will make sense to you too.

Give yourself time and be gentle with yourself and your family. No one and nothing is perfect in this life, but we are getting ready to return to the spirit world where we are a bit less fettered by the rules. In this life and in the spirit world you are deeply, truly, genuinely loved. You are a wonderful little boy.

With much love,
Grandmom

Here are symbols for some of the major religions of the world. There are many others, and there are minor branches of many as well. We can learn from all cultures of the world. Similarly each belief system deserves respect.
Fotosearch image used with permission.

A POEM BY MARIGOLD

Dear Bowen,

This is a very different kind of letter. I am going to introduce you to a very dear friend of mine. Her name is Marigold (JoAnne) Klemmer. She is a close friend who knows me very well. She is a very intelligent woman. Her thoughts are clear, compassionate, kind, and directed by her close relationship with the divine.

Her poem, included here, is a metaphor intended to help us understand the relationship of humanity with avarice, power, and fear. It is meant for grownups. I include it here trusting that you will read all of your letters as you are ready. Perhaps your mommy and daddy will help you understand the symbolism here. Perhaps you will help them understand some of these concepts. I say that because being a mom has helped me understand many concepts I could not fathom before I had children. Having grandchildren has taken me to a deeper level than I thought possible. "And the little children will lead us."

I am including this poem just as Marigold wrote it. I hope you can glean, in reading her thoughts here, the depth of her love and faith.

A BEGINNING

By Marigold (JoAnne) Klemmer

I told my friend I'd seen the Idol
And he said
 "I'll have to think about that".
I told my father and he said
  "So what's your point?"
"The Idol must be destroyed!" I said,
And he said
  "But who will feed us?"

And I had no answer.

So I searched for a wise man
To answer the question.
I found a preacher.
And he said
     "There are no Idols anymore".
And then a lawyer.
And he said
     "For thousands of dollars, we'll sue the state".
And I said
     "I have no money".
And he said
     "You have no case".

So I asked the doctor
And he said
     "Isn't it wonderful what science can do?"
And I said
     "What about the Idol?"
And he said
     "It's irrelevant!"

By now I was beginning to doubt what I'd seen
So I looked again.
This time the Idol was surrounded by priests
Leading the worship.
And many brought sacrifices.
Off to one side was a group of children.
I wondered why they were there.
They weren't dancing.
They weren't singing.
Off to the side
They seemed to be waiting.
Their eyes were full of expectation

As if for a promise to be fulfilled.
There was something familiar about the scene.
Something I couldn't place.
(Later, I wondered why the things I had seen
Were hidden to everyone else.)

So for a while I denied what I'd seen.
I lived my life,
Collected my stuff,
Until I noticed
The children were changing.
They still played and laughed
But what was that thing
They all seemed to carry?
So I asked them
And they said
      "Our inhalers, of course!"
And ran away to play
While they could still breathe.

So I returned to the wise men
And the preacher said
      "Liberal politics weaken the nation!"
And the lawyer said
      "All you need is thousands of dollars".

And I said
      "Or what?"
And he said
      "Or you're wasting my time".

So I went back to the doctor
And he said
      "Doing drugs ruins the genes!"
I asked,

"Is there no other answer?"
And he said
"None we can face".
And I went away and pondered some more.

Again I came upon the place of the priests.
The children were no longer off to the side.
The priests were offering them drinks from the chalice
And in their innocence
They drank.
But it wasn't wine.
And it wasn't water.
They drank the fluid that flowed
From the Idol.
And it glowed
And it stank
And one by one
The children fell
As the blood of the Idol
Mixed
With the blood of the innocent.
And I wanted to save them
But it was too late.
And I raged at the Idol

Safely
From behind the bushes.
And then I saw
That these would be replaced
By thousands of others.
From everywhere.
From all time.
And I knew in my heart
That the Idol
Must be killed.

So I went back to my friend

And said "Will you help me?"
And he said
        "I'm afraid."
"But will you help me?"
        "I'll lose my job, and my stuff."
And I said,
        "Does it matter?"
And he said
        "Yes."
So I asked my father
And he said,
        "What will my friends think?"
And I said,
        "Does it matter?"
And he said,
        "Yes."
So I searched for a partner
And found that I had none
And I asked myself,
        "Does it matter?"
And the answer was
        "No."
If there are no others,
I'll do it myself.

With love from Marigold

_____

Although I did not write this poem, I offer it here as a story whose time will come, as you grow. I have read it many times in the years since Marigold wrote it, and I seem to appreciate the depth of it more each time.

I hope you will eventually come to appreciate it too.

In addition, I hope you will grow in the understanding that when situations are unhealthy, if no one will help you improve the status quo, you may need to try to change it by yourself.

Remember too, that your family is willing to stand with you when you need help. Never be afraid to ask.

With much love,
Grandmom

Here is a picture of Marigold and her family.
(Missing from the photo is her beloved son, Joseph, who has returned to the spirit world.)
From left to right: Sammy, Marigold, John Paul, Grace, and Christopher.

TWO FAMILY HEROS

Dear Bowen,

This is a story about my mother (your great Grandmom) and my brother (your Great Uncle Tav). This true story will give you a little more information about some of your ancestors. My mother was a quiet sort of person with a wonderful sense of humor and a good heart. She tried always to be kind. My brother was much the same in those ways, except he was not always quiet. He loved music as I did, so we often played guitars and sang together. We sometimes became rather boisterous in our singing. Aside from that, he was rather quiet.

One time we went swimming in the Schuylkill River near Reading, PA. Tav was there as was my Mother. We were all standing on the bottom of the river with the water about waist to chest high. We were talking, joking, and playing in the water. Suddenly Tav stepped off a ledge under the water. He did not know the ledge was there, nor did any of the rest of us. Tav looked as if he were still playing in the water, kicking and splashing about, but Mother knew better. She very quickly swam to him, put her hand under his chin, told him to lie still. She swam back to the shallow part where we were standing, pulling him back to the place where he could stand again. He was still in the water, but not close to the ledge. Mother had recognized that he could not regain his balance in the water, and was in danger of drowning. Tav was a bit shaken by that adventure, and shortly thereafter he got out of the water. Mother was still very calm. She was a good swimmer and knew about life saving techniques from her youth when she swam in a pool near her home in West Reading. Tav did not know she was a good swimmer; after that day he said she was a <u>great</u> swimmer. She saved his life that day.

That could have been enough of a story, but there is a postscript. Many years later, Mother and Tav and a few other people were having dinner in a restaurant. Midway through the meal Mother got up and walked away. Tav immediately realized she had left the table without excusing herself. She NEVER did that. She was polite to a fault. So Tav got up and followed her. He caught up with her outside the restaurant. He stopped her and asked if she were OK. She shook her head "no." He asked if she could speak. Again, she indicated "no." Tav had been trained in first aid and he had asked the right questions. He quickly performed the Heimlich Maneuver and she coughed up the piece of food on which she had been choking. They walked back to the restaurant together. Now they had each saved the life of the other.

They seldom spoke of these incidents, but I never forgot about them. I wonder how often we do a good deed and no one ever knows. Sometimes we help people and we do not even realize how important our actions are until long after, or perhaps we never know. Still, it is important for us to do our best to help others when we can.

You are a helpful little boy. I know you helped your Mommy stir the vegetables for the vegetarian lasagna we had at your house for our Christmas (eve) dinner. Your Mommy and Daddy and all the rest of your family are very proud of you.

With much love,
Grandmom

Here you are helping your Mommy and Daddy cook.
You have always been a very helpful little boy.
Thank you for all you do.

Here is a picture of our two family heros; my Mother (your Great Grandmom) and my brother, (your Great Uncle Tav). The photo was taken in the back yard of my Grandmom's house, where I lived for happy years when I was a child. This photo was taken around 1955, near the time when Mother saved Tav.

HEAD START IN THE UPPER PENINSULA OF MICHIGAN

Dear Bowen,

In the late 1960s I was a VISTA Volunteer in the upper peninsula of Michigan. Michigan, as you will see if you look on a map, is two peninsulas stretching into the great lakes. The lower peninsula is the one most well known. It looks like a mitten with the thumb in Lake Huron and the fingers in Lake Michigan. The upper peninsula is pointed east and is connected at its base in Wisconsin. It is bordered on the north by Lake Superior and on the south by Lake Michigan. At one time the upper peninsula, known by the locals as the UP, was so highly prized a war was fought over it. This was because of the minerals in the ground (copper and iron) and the huge virgin stands of trees. Many masts for great ships were made from the tall straight trees from those forests. Ohio lost the war and Michigan won, so the UP is part of Michigan, not Ohio. Nor is it part of Wisconsin, which would make lots more sense.

The tragedy of the tale is this. The companies which bought the land after the war was over, lumber companies and mining companies, took ore out of the land and cut the big, strong trees without planting new ones. It takes many years for a big forest to grow. When the companies had taken all they wanted from the land they stopped paying taxes on it. They just moved on. The land therefore reverted to the state and no taxes were collected for many years. That might sound like a good idea, but in fact the lack of a tax base caused suffering for the people since the state did not have enough tax revenue for good schools, roads, and similar necessities.

This is not, however, a story about unethical business practices. It is a story about parents' love for their children, regardless of their circumstances. As a Vista Volunteer I worked on a few projects. One was initiating a welfare rights group, another was a public health project for which I tested hundreds of children for tuberculosis (tuberculoses was and may still be endemic in the UP). The last was recruiting children for Head Start. This is the subject of our story.

Head Start is a program for pre-school children who are from poor families. These families do not have money to buy lots of toys for their children. Often the children have neither books nor educational toys. You have cards to help you learn numbers, letters, and words. Cards, books, certain DVDs, some puzzles, et cetera, are considered educational toys. I am so proud of you when I see you name the objects on the cards and say the numbers you see there. The children who go to Head Start are able to play with educational toys and so learn about letters and numbers.

As a Vista Volunteer I learned about a family living in a tar-paper shack in the woods. I set out to find them. I was told to call out to them because they were living on government land. They were worried about being arrested for "squatting." That is what they call living on land which belongs to the government. Somehow I found the shack and called out to the folks there. The father came out and we talked for a little while, then I was invited into the shack; their home.

There was one room with a cot in a corner. There were a few shelves with dishes and there was a wood stove in the middle for heat and for cooking. It was late autumn and quite cold. The children, two little girls, were quietly sitting on the cot. Each had a hand-sewn doll. They had no books at all. There were a few straight back chairs. There was no electricity. They had a battery-powered radio. I could hardly believe the abject poverty I saw there. The family was gracious and hospitable. They offered me a cup of coffee. Not wishing to offend them, I accepted. There was no sink or running water. In the winter their water came from melting snow. There is a lot of snow in the UP, more than 200 inches of snow each winter. When there was no snow the Father walked miles to a stream and carried water back to the shack in a bucket. The Mom took water from the bucket to put a pan with water on the stove. It quickly boiled. She put some instant coffee in a child's plastic cup and put hot water into it. I thanked her. The water was so hot it partially melted the plastic. I drank the coffee, grateful for the kindness of this family who gave of the little they had.

We talked about Head Start and I told them I knew they loved their children and wanted the best for them. I asked them if they thought it important for the girls to learn to read. Yes, they truly wanted their girls to learn to read. They wanted their children to have a better life than they had lived thus far. So I asked if they would consider allowing their children to go to Head Start. They had lots of questions and I answered them as well as I could. They finally agreed the program would be good for their children. They would send them. The only problem was getting them to the school bus stop. It was far from their shack. I will make sure they get there, their Father promised.

In fact their Father did make sure the children got to Head Start. There was so much snow every winter he could not even walk through the snow for that distance when he was alone. But love makes all things possible. He walked a long way to the school bus stop every morning on home made snow shoes with the girls on his shoulders so they could not only see books, but touch them and begin to unravel the mystery of those marks on the pages which were letters arranged to make words.

They went to Head Start the whole year and they were scheduled to start kindergarten the next year. My Vista year was over, and I had left the UP of Michigan. I never heard how they did then but I know they had a Head Start for school, just as you are getting; not from the Head Start program, but from your Mommy and Daddy who love you so much. When you read one of your books, sometimes think of those children who had never touched a book. Those who allowed their mommy to melt their little cup to offer coffee to a stranger and so open the door to a new world. Remember mommies and daddies love their children even when they have little to offer them. Even when "everything" is so little, the ultimate gift is love.

This is a true story about a few of the beautiful people I have been honored to meet so far in my life. What a great lesson for me to see how they lived and loved each other in their little shack in the woods. How generous they were with the little they had!

With much love,
Grandmom

You are a fortunate little boy, since you have many toys with which to play.
In this photograph you are swinging on a little swing at the beach near your house.

Here you are playing in the forest, as I used to do at my Aunt Ruth's house.
You were very little here, so your parents were with you on this day at the park.

GRANDMOM'S WALK WITH MAGGIE

Dear Bowen,

Four days ago I had a little adventure at Mount Holyoke College. You may remember when your Mommy, Daddy, Ozzie, Maggie, you and I went for a walk around that campus last summer. I think it was Ozzie who found the trail which goes all the way around a lake there. I have walked around that path many times since then, and usually Maggie goes with me. She loves to go for a walk and she is quite familiar with the path. When she gets out of the car she has to "heel" for a time until we get to the part of the trail which is little traveled. That is so she does not interfere with students or other folk who are walking there, nor be in danger from cars. When we reach the part where there is little foot traffic and no cars at all, I stop, she sits, as dogs are supposed to do when on the "heel" command. I tell her she is a good dog and then take the leash off her collar. She sits waiting. Then I say the word which must be one of her favorite sounds; "Free!" Then off she goes running ahead of me along the path with which she is so familiar.

Our walk last Sunday, where our adventure transpired, began as usual. She was happily running ahead of me, then back again. She does not like to have much distance between us. Of course she can run much faster than I can walk, so she runs many times the distance I cover in the same amount of time. The trees and grass were full of good smells which she drank in as she stopped and sniffed waiting for me to catch up. Then she was off running again as I continued to walk at my own pace.

All went as expected until near the end of the path. We had gone nearly all the way around the lake when the muddy path morphed into a sheet of ice. The ice had been melting, but it was still several inches thick at that part of the path. The day was fairly warm, so there was a bit of ice melt on top of the ice which made it even more slippery than it would have been if it had been dry. My skills do not include a good sense of balance, and I was woefully inadequate at walking on the ice. In fact, I knew I would not be able to cross the large portion of the path which for me was impassible. I thought of going around the icy patch on the path, but one side ended at the lake and the other went up a steep hill covered with ice. Neither side allowed me to find solid footing, so I found myself, unable to take steps in any direction, clinging to a tree.

I thought maybe Maggie could help me, although on second thought, what could Maggie do? She is just a little dog, and I am a big person. She could not carry me, nor could she move the ice away from the path. Still, I called her to heel. She came right away, but instead of sitting near me as she usually does when called, she positioned herself right up against my left leg, almost leaning on it. She often leans to one side when

46

she stands for any length of time to take her weight off her right rear leg which was broken when she was a puppy. She performed this maneuver although it had her leaning the wrong way, with her weight to her right side rather than the left. She stayed there and looked into my face. I put my left hand on her shoulders and said "heel" again. I put as little weight on her as possible, lest I hurt her.

What a remarkable little girl she proved to be. She took one step forward and waited for me to slip and slide until I caught up to her at that little distance. When I was stable and not sliding, she took one more step and waited again for me to get my footing. With my hand on her shoulders I was able to slide a bit, but maintain my balance. It took a long time, but she never turned her attention away from her self appointed task. She continued this pattern for a long time, until we were on solid footing, past the ice. Then she turned and looked at me again; she looked pleased. I was not only happy to be on solid ground, I was thrilled at Maggie's brilliant performance. She somehow knew I needed help. Incredibly, she knew what I needed. She never hesitated to do what needed to be done.

I am so proud of her. She is a healing dog in many ways. The rest of our walk was unremarkable, but I am still thinking of what she did. I am also wondering, how did she know I needed help? How did she know what to do? My theory, which I cannot prove, is that dogs are more connected to the energy in the universe and in the world than most people. That connection allowed the needed information to enter her little brain. She acted with caring and love to help me. I am hoping to be able to be similarly connected and as willing to do what I can to help others who may need to lean on a shoulder as I did.

May you always have a shoulder appear when you need one, even when you least expect it. May you continue to be a helper when you are able, just as you are in your music class when you help all the children clean up. I am proud of you too, dear Bowen.

With much love,
Grandmom

This is Maggie in one of the parks where she likes to play.
You may notice how she sits, without bending her right knee.
Although she does not have good range of motion in that leg,
she has enough heart to compensate for that, and more.

HEARTBEATS

—

Dear Bowen,

Some time ago I began to develop an interest in the metaphysical. That means things not necessarily seen, but probably true. An example would be certain concepts; for example, love. Another example might be certain spiritual theories. Auras are one metaphysical concept, as is Reiki.

I studied the theories of auras, chakras, physics, and the workings of a computer program which I have used for imaging and interpreting auras. With practice I have learned to see auras without the computer program. The appearance of a person's aura can indicate the health of that person and sometimes the degree of spirit in her/his life. One must be careful in interpreting the appearance of a person's aura. It is not meant to be a diagnostic practice, although it can give an indication of general health and wellness.

I also received training in Reiki, achieving the level of Master. Reiki is intended to intensify the energy flowing through a person to elevate their level of health. Practicing and receiving Reiki has opened some doors and concepts for me which otherwise might be closed. Since I have taught Reiki with my Reiki Master, I am also able to teach Reiki. I would be happy to teach you if you develop an interest in that kind of energy work.

Another area in which I received training is facilitating drum circles. I have had some success in each of these areas, but the activity most interesting to me is drumming. I most often use African drums called Djembes. There are other kinds too, which I will show you as time goes by. When I have room to display my drums you will be able to decide each time you visit, which one you might want to play.

As a way of putting these interests together, I formed a little company called "Heartbeats". Your Daddy helped me with this project, and as part of his help he designed a logo for the company. The logo has three parts. First is a drum, which of course represents drumming, especially group drumming. The drum in the logo is a Native American drum, sometimes called a frame drum, buffalo drum, or "calling" drum. Almost every culture uses some kind of drum similar to the buffalo drum. It is interesting that worldwide, over many years, not a single anthropologist nor paleontologist has found a single civilization which does not use drums in some way. Most cultures use drums to communicate, to celebrate, and to grieve.

The second part of the logo is a hand with Japanese words on the palm. The words are "REI" meaning universal or divine, and "KI" meaning life force. This represents the study and practice of Reiki. The Japanese concept of KI is also taught in China, although the Chinese word for life force is CHI. The energy is the same.

The colors around the drum represent the third part of the logo. Those colors represent the aura. Some people can see auras around other people, around themselves, animals, plants, or objects. Energy, or life force is in everything. This is my opinion, although many others may not agree with that. You will decide for your self how much if any energy is in various animate and inanimate objects as you encounter them.

Your Daddy has encouraged me in all areas of my life. May you grow in those good qualities as your Daddy has. His caring, being, loving, and playing are inspirational. Your are much like your Daddy, dear Bowen, and I am very grateful for both of you.

With much love,
Grandmom

This is the logo which was designed by your Daddy.
I love the colors and the symbolism in this work of art.

BIG BROTHER BOWEN

Dear Bowen,

Some time ago your Mommy and Daddy told you that your little family was going to grow a bit. A baby was going to be born, who was to be your baby brother. It took some time for Mommy and Daddy to decide what the baby's name would be. Finally we started thinking of the baby as "August".

You noticed that Mommy's belly was getting big. You knew that was because the baby who was in there, getting ready to be born, was growing bigger. While the baby was growing there were other preparations to be made.

You, being so grown up, did not need a crib any longer. So your Mommy and Daddy bought you a big boy bed. It was in the shape of a fire engine, and you loved it. You were proud to sleep in a big boy bed, and we were all proud of you.

The crib was moved into the other room upstairs. That room is now August's room. The safari theme moved into that room too. Your room had new decals and decorations installed, reflecting your passion for cars, trucks, and especially fire trucks. Your books stayed. Many of your toy cars and trucks were put on a shelf in your room since you are old enough now to play in your room upstairs.

After a long time your Mommy knew it was time for August to be born. Grandma Janer came to take care of you at home. I met your parents at the hospital. Your Daddy was there. The midwife was there. Of course your Mommy was there. And after a time August was there too. He was a beautiful baby, as you were. He did not make your Mommy wait long before making his appearance. Your Mommy held him and talked to him as she had held you after you were born. Your Daddy and I were standing beside the bed admiring August and your Mommy. The midwife asked your Daddy if he wanted to cut August's umbilical cord. That is the connection which becomes the belly button after babies are born. Your Daddy said no. Many non-medical people do not like to do things like that. Then the midwife asked me. Being a nurse, I did not mind so I said yes. It was quite special being able to cut his umbilical cord. In case you are wondering, one of the nurses cut your umbilical cord because you needed some procedures to help you get started breathing on your own when you were born. August was able to do that by himself.

You and your brother are as closely related as two people can be. August's DNA, the composition of one's biological heritage is closer to your DNA than it is to either of your parents. He will, as time passes, be closer to you than to anyone else in life. Likewise you will be closer to him than to anyone else. It is very special, having a brother.

Phone calls were made, and everyone wanted to come see the new Tullo. Your Grandma Janer also wanted to see her new grandson. But she thoughtfully wanted to bring a gift. She took you shopping and let you pick a gift for your baby brother. Do you remember what gift you chose for August? You picked a white seal, exactly like yours. At the time his seal was bigger than he was. It was very nice of you to pick a gift like the one you have and love so much. It was wonderful for your Grandma Janer to take you shopping for a gift for your new little brother.

Your Daddy took a blanket which had been wrapped around August home and gave it to Ozzie, as he had done after you were born. That is because dogs recognize their world by smells more than by seeing. So when August came home Ozzie recognized his smell and knew immediately that August was part of the family. Your Daddy is very smart, and very kind. He thought of Ozzie and helped him perceive the new family member in a way he could understand.

When you came to visit Mommy and August you were wearing your new shirt. It says, "Big Brother" on the front. I notice you sometimes wear that shirt even though you have been a big brother for a long time now, for almost ten months. You may or may not have thought of this. No matter where you and your baby brother may go throughout your lives, <u>you will always be August's Big Brother</u>. Awesome!

With much love,
Grandmom

Here you are greeting your new baby brother August. He was only a few hours old, and you were learning to be gentle with him.

Here is August with his gift Seal, just like yours. Many thanks to your Grandma Janer for taking you shopping for your baby brother.

Here you are wearing your "big brother" shirt. You are waiting patiently for August to grow big enough to play with you.

Here is a picture of your Grandma Janer with August. He is wide awake in this picture. His hair has a little red tint, to please his Grandpa.

UNCLE TAV'S TRANSITION

Dear Bowen,

This is a true story about your Great Aunt Evelyn and your Great Uncle Tav. Tav was my brother, and Evelyn my sister-in-law. I say "was" because my Brother returned to the spirit world January 25, 1993. This was just a few days before Tav and Evelyn's 37th wedding anniversary. It was very significant, since they had been together for a long time, and were extraordinarily devoted to each other. Although all the family have been sad about Tav's death, we have also been happy that Tav returned to the spirit world. He was in great pain prior to his return there. Although we knew we would miss him greatly, we were relieved and happy that he was no longer suffering. But I am getting ahead of my story.

Tav called me himself to give me the news that the biopsy which was taken from his adrenal gland showed that he had lung cancer. The cells in his adrenal gland were abnormal lung cells. Malignant cells. These words were frightening to all of us. Still, Tav was as brave and optimistic as could be expected, having just received such news. On the advice of his doctor he updated his will, his health care proxy, his advanced directives, and his durable power of attorney. These are important documents for adults to have ready, regardless of the state of their health. Children do not need to concern themselves about that. Tav was preparing to turn his affairs over to his wife and children so if or when he could not speak for himself, they would know what he wanted.

Tav had chosen to have chemotherapy using the most modern agents available. When he had his treatments he would be hospitalized for a day. On those occasions I would take a day or two off from work. I would go sit with him in the hospital. We had a little joke, long standing, which we played out every time I visited, long before he got sick. He would always greet me with a hug and a kiss. He would say, "You came all this way to see me" and I would answer, "It was either that or clean the house." He would say, "I win that one, hands down." We would laugh at our clever repartee, then sit down to have coffee and conversation.

After two or three chemotherapy treatments Tav went to have a repeat body scan to determine the effectiveness of the treatments. The news was not good. In the beginning he had three tumors in his chest and one in his abdomen. After treatment, it was no longer possible to count the tumors. There were clusters of tumors. His doctor suggested a few options for Tav, who chose to come home and stop treatment. His family supported him in his decision. He then had hospice care. He was given medication to help ease his pain. He had lots of pain, regardless of the medicine. I called him nearly every day, and as he got sicker I called every day. I talked first to Evelyn, who answered the phone, then she would give the phone to Tav so I could talk to him. It was on a Thursday when Evelyn said he did not want to talk on the phone any more. He had so little lung function it was very difficult for him to talk. I told Evelyn I was going to come to see him that day.

I was at work when that conversation took place, so I went to see my boss. I had told her that Tav was sick, with a poor prognosis. I told her on this occasion that I was going to go to Pennsylvania to see him and I was going to stay until "it is over". She said, "You can't do that!" I told her I knew she was my boss and I respected her position. I told her I knew she would have to do whatever she needed to do, including disciplinary steps. She could have had me fired. I told her while she did what she thought necessary, I would do what I needed to do, and that was to be with my brother. "I will be with him as long as I can be." I told her I would call her as the situation changed. She watched me walk away.

So I went to be with him. When I came into the house he could not get up to greet me, and he did not start our standard script. Instead, he asked me, "How long can you stay?" I told him, "I'm here for the duration." He just said "good". I realized he was concerned about Evelyn. He was glad I was there to help her get through this difficult time. Their children were supportive as well. Joy was there because she was able to be away from her job. Mark, who had a very hard time getting another doctor to cover his office, would come every day after office hours. Ken, at the time was a bank manager. Ken went over finances, insurance, etc with Tav so he could set up the finances for Evelyn. Then she would not have to worry about how to handle financial things alone. Tav had taken very good care of her long before he knew he was sick.

As Tav got sicker and weaker, it was more and more difficult for him to talk. On one occasion Tav had asked for water because he was very thirsty. He was not eating any longer. He was not hungry, he could not swallow solid food; eventually he could not even swallow jello. I was on my way into the room when Evelyn came out in tears. She said to me, "Oh, Alice, we are kinder to cats and dogs than we are to people." It was very hard to see him suffer and not be able to help him. He simply could not swallow the water, so we could not relieve his thirst. I told Evelyn that we could relieve some of his thirst by giving him intravenous fluids, but I reminded her that he had said he did not want that. Hydration would prolong his life. Not having IV fluids was in his advance directive as well. Evelyn remembered that, she was just so hoping there would be something to do to make him more comfortable. I offered the only suggestion I could. Since he could no longer push the button on his morphine drip, we could do that every ten minutes to give him more pain relief. It would help him be more comfortable. It would also slow his heart rate and help him return to the spirit world more quickly. She went to push the button.

Joy, Evelyn, and I took turns sitting with him. During the night one of us would sleep and the others would stay with him. We were all tired, but we wanted to spend every possible minute with him. Every time one of us would go out of the room we would tell him we were going for coffee, a bathroom break, a shower, etc. He would say, "I love you." He wanted us to be with him. We would tell him we loved him too.

On one occasion I was with him when both Evelyn and Joy were busy with errands in the house. Tav said he wanted to talk to me about something. He told me people were telling him to "let go" and he was trying to do that, but it was not working. "What am I doing wrong?" I wanted to give him a good answer, but I did not know what to say. So I tried not to think, but to listen. This little story came to me as I said it to him. "Tav, this reminds me quite a lot of childbirth." "Childbirth, what are you talking about?" He sounded annoyed, thinking I was being silly. I went on, "Well, you are in a ton of pain. In my memory childbirth is like that. We have nothing to say about when it starts and when it stops We cannot make it progress faster nor slower. We just have to go along with it. And in both cases, we are looking forward to a new life." "Oh," he said, "then I am doing all right." I wanted to say yes, but I had started to cry. Tav lost consciousness at that point. He may have fallen asleep from exhaustion. Regardless, that was the last real conversation we ever had in this life. I look forward to seeing him in the spirit world and asking him to tell me about his childbirth experience.

I was sleeping when Joy came into the room to wake me. I worried I had slept too long, but Joy told me I had only been asleep for about 20 minutes. She told me his breathing was different. I had asked her to look for that. In fact he was having Chene Stokes respirations, a sign that death is imminent. I told Joy and Evelyn but they had concluded the time was near themselves. We held his hands and talked to him a little; we told him we loved him. We told him we would take care of each other. His breathing became slower and slower and finally stopped. It was still dark, early in the morning.

Evelyn jumped up to call the hospice nurse as she had been instructed to do. The nurse said she would be there within the hour. Evelyn looked around for something she could do. I offered the suggestion we could bathe him. She jumped at the thought. So we bathed him in the bed. It was a moment of sharing with Evelyn that I will never forget. I think that is when it became firmly fixed in my mind that she truly is my sister. Evelyn called her sons and they came. Everyone had some task which he or she wanted to do to honor Tav. We all drank coffee. Evelyn cooked.

I remember standing at the kitchen sink, realizing the sun was coming up. I had always said the sun rose and set on my brother. I always looked up to him. It was not only because he was older than I by about three and a half years. It was how my world was ordered. I could hardly believe the sun could come up as if nothing had happened. It rained hard that morning. Perhaps the sky was weeping with us. Tav, who had a great sense of humor, may have helped us see some silly things throughout that difficult time. So we cried together, we laughed together as well. "The saving grace of a gentle humor. (MMJ)"

Evelyn, having been his wife for a very long time, said it is not only that he was such a huge part of her life; he was her life. I could see that. I see it still when I talk to her. She still cooks for us when we go visit her. When she makes chili she always hands me a bowl of chili and a serving of shredded cheese. "Here," she says, "Your brother liked it like that." So he did. So do I.

Later that day, if memory serves me correctly we all went to the funeral parlor to choose a casket. Our mother had died fifteen months earlier. Tav had told Evelyn he wanted the same casket. This was so Evelyn would not have to be concerned about that decision. When we looked at what seemed a zillion caskets, she told me she was not sure about getting a casket like Mother's. Evelyn liked a different one, but she did not want to go against his wishes. I told her Tav was trying to make the decision easier for her by suggesting a casket like Mother's, not harder. I told her if she likes something else better, there was no one in the family who would object. All of us cheered her decision, so she had the one she wanted for him. There is a little funny story about that, but it is for another time.

I had called my boss on Monday morning, the day Tav died. She was amazed that I called so soon. I guess she thought I might have been planning to take off for months or more. She obviously did not know me very well. She had only recently been made my supervisor. She offered her sympathy. The staff where I worked sent flowers and they contributed money for the church were Tav had belonged, where he and Evelyn had wed, where his funeral services were held. The donations paid for a vigil light. It hangs in the sanctuary of the church. Sometimes when I go to Pennsylvania I go look at it, sometimes I touch it.

I returned to Connecticut in time for work the following Monday. There was a large hole inside my heart, a Tav shaped hole. My friends were kind to me. Many of them spent time with me, listening to the story I needed to tell. Cathy, especially empathetic and kind, listened to my story over and over again. Although nothing can ever fill that hole, the edges have worn more smooth with time. It is still painful, but more bearable. We are more used to it now, but nothing can replace Evelyn's beloved husband. Nothing can replace my brother. Although this is a sad story, there is good in it too. Tav still lives in the spirit world. As you know, that is where we all come from in the first place.

May you and your spouse, if you choose to marry, share a great love as Tav and Evelyn have done. May you and your baby brother share a great love as Tav and I have. May your love sustain you all your life. May you have fun in good times as well as in difficult times. May you know that your family is here for you every day. Always.

With much love,
Grandmom

This is a good picture of Tav. He is standing as usual,
with his head to the side, hands on his hips, and a nice grin on his face.
This photo was given to me by Joy, and I thank her for it.

MAGGIE GOES TO A CONCERT

Dear Bowen,

This is a story about Maggie. You remember her I am sure. She is a medium size dog, not as big as your Ozzie, but a good size for her. She is black with long silky hair, floppy ears, and a wagging tail. Like most dogs, Maggie likes to go for walks. Like Ozzie, she is sufficiently trustworthy so that she can go off leash if the area is free of cars and other dangerous things.

Last summer I was walking Maggie on the campus of Mount Holyoke College in South Hadley, MA. You have walked there too. In fact it was on a walk there with you and your mommy and daddy that Ozzie found that nice walking path around the lake. Maggie and I have walked around the lake many times since then. There is a story about that too, but it is a story for another time. This story is about an unexpected adventure for Maggie.

On this occasion, because it was summer, there were not many students at the college. We walked all around the gardens and across the quad, enjoying the fine day. Since there were so few people, and since Maggie never goes far from me, I let her off leash. She bounded ahead, keeping me in sight. This is also her usual behavior. As your mommy can confirm, I sometimes become distracted watching a bird or squirrel; on this occasion I did just that. I lost track of Maggie, who suddenly disappeared. I thought she may have gone behind some shrubbery and assumed she would come back when she realized I was not with her. It turned out there was a building with an open door, and she had gone into the building. I walked over to the building and found that the open door led into a beautiful church. Maggie had gone right in, not realizing dogs are usually not welcome in churches. Not only that, there was a concert in progress inside the church. There was a choir singing for people in the town. The college puts on many programs like that either for free or for a donation or a small ticket fee. This one was free. The alumni choir was giving a farewell performance before going on a year-long tour of China. The choir members were quite talented. If not for Maggie I would have missed the entire concert.

Maggie had no idea it was a church or that dogs are not usually welcomed in church. But she seemed to enjoy the music as well as the rest of us. When I first saw her in there, she was trotting down the center aisle of the church toward me. Her tail was wagging and her tongue was lolling out of her mouth, making her look as if she were smiling. The most amazing thing to me is the reaction of the audience. No one moved to get her out of the church, in fact, few people even looked at her. Those who did were smiling. They must have concluded, as I did, that she is a dog who enjoys a good tune as well as anyone else. It was amazing to me that no one reacted to her presence there. No one mentioned to me that she was in the church. That is probably one of the reasons I like Western Massachusetts so well. People are generally quite flexible and accepting of the unusual, even a dog enjoying a concert in a church.

May you too be accepting of the unusual and unexpected events which occur in your life. May most of those things be happy, like concerts and well behaved dogs. For those things which are unpleasant, may you have your dog, your family, and your sense of humor to sustain you.

Remember we are always there for you because you are part of our family and we truly love you. Maggie and Ozzie too!

With much love,
Grandmom

Here is Maggie resting in the park after a long run.
No concerts on this day, however.
Maybe next time….

THE FISHWAY

Dear Bowen,

This is a true story about a special kind of creatures who live in the water. You know about these animals; they are FISH. You have several toy fish in your collection, and they are different colors. This story, however, is about real fish and how they try to live their lives in the waters nearby.

The Connecticut River begins in Canada, flows south between Vermont and New Hampshire, through Massachusetts and Connecticut, and into the ocean. The word Connecticut is a Native American word. It means "long tidal river". The river does change with the tide, just as the salt marsh behind your house changes. It is considered a river rather than a stream or creek because it is more than one hundred miles long. This river is quite near my house here in South Hadley. It separates South Hadley from its near neighbor to the southwest, Holyoke, MA. Now let us move on to the fish.

Years ago people started building dams across rivers for various reasons. Some of those reasons include: irrigation for crops, "storing" water in artificial lakes called "reservoirs", and hydroelectric power. The root word of hydro means water, so hydroelectric power is electricity generated by water. A dam is built across the river with a hole built into it. The water is forced through the hole in the dam where a generator is located. The generator has big blades, rather like fan blades. Water moves the blades as the water flows through them. The blades move the generator parts and electricity is the result. The water continues through the special hole in the dam down the river, and the electricity flows along wires to our homes and businesses.

The fish involved here are species of fish which live part of their lives in the ocean and part of their lives in the river. They are hatched or born in a river. When they are old enough they go to the ocean to live most of their lives. When they are mature they return to the river in which they were spawned (born) and have their own babies.

This is the problem caused by the dams. The fish can leap over the dam to go downstream, but the dam is much too high to jump upstream. If the fish cannot get upstream to lay their eggs there will be no baby fish and no future adult fish. The species will disappear, a process we call extinction. One species which had become extinct over the past several years is the Connecticut River Atlantic Salmon. This is a fish which has in the past spawned far north in the Connecticut River but could not get upstream to spawn. There were no more Atlantic Salmon in the Connecticut River nor any Connecticut River Salmon in the Atlantic Ocean.

The good news is that a law was passed in the United States that there could be no dams blocking the movement of migrating fish. That meant the dams built in the future AND the dams already built had to make some way for fish to move upstream. A few different ways were considered. One used elsewhere is a "fish ladder". This is a structure much like a ladder lying down in the water. The fish can leap up one rung at a time, get to the top, then over the dam. The fish continue their journey upstream. This method was not used at our dam.

For one thing, the Connecticut River Atlantic Salmon were already extinct. So the scientists who study fish had an idea. They captured Atlantic Salmon which had spawned elsewhere. These fish were taken to hatcheries to spawn. The fry (a name given to newly hatched fish) were kept safely in the hatchery until they got to a fair size and then were taken far upstream in the Connecticut River and were "seeded" into the river. That means the fish were put into the river with the hope they would go to the ocean to live most of their adult life, then come back as adult fish swim up the Connecticut River, then spawn. There was no evidence this scheme would work, but the scientists tried it.

The next part of this story is about the way the fish which spawn upstream do get past our dam. The method is called a "fishway". We can go visit the fishway when you come visit in the spring. On one side of the dam is a special outlet where the water coming out is the same temperature and same speed as the water moving downstream. So the fish go into the outlet thinking they are going upstream. Of course they cannot get out of the outlet after they get in there. That may sound like a very bad thing for the fish, but it is not a bad thing at all.

A big bucket comes up under the fish, picks them up along with water, then lifts them to the level of the dam in one big step. Now they are not quite past the dam, but they are well on their way. There is a very big glass tank which leads upstream, but the fish cannot get out of there either. The reason the fish are there is so they do not get caught in the current and go back over the dam (downstream) again. While the fish swim through the big glass tank they are identified and counted. People such as ourselves can go see the fish as they swim in the tank. The tank is called the fishway. After the fish are counted and identified they are allowed to swim all the way to the end of the tank. The end is opened so the fish swim out into the river again, far upstream from the dam. Now they can continue their journey upstream, lay their eggs and have their baby fish. On my first two visits to the fishway I saw several species of fish but no Atlantic Salmon. I did, however, see two moray eels, one on each visit.

Here is the best news. For the past few years the people who study the fish, identify them, and count them, have begun to see and count Atlantic Salmon. Since they are swimming upstream to have their babies, they are now considered Connecticut River Atlantic Salmon. So if this trend continues, the scientists will for the first time in history, have reintroduced a species which had become extinct. Of course the Atlantic Salmon itself was not extinct, just the subspecies which spawned in the Connecticut River. I find it exciting regardless, as do those fish identifier/counter people I met at the fishway.

What do you think of that fishway, Bowen? I very much enjoyed my two visits last summer, and I am looking forward to going again to see the fish. Next spring in May I hope to be able to see the fishway with my dear grandson – YOU! Perhaps we will be able to take your mommy and daddy to see the fishway too.

With much love,
Grandmom

These are Atlantic Salmon Fry.
They still have their egg yolk attached and will live on that food for a year.

Adolescent Atlantic Salmon are called "smolt".
This is the age when they begin their journey to the sea.

These Atlantic Salmon are adults.
We hope we will soon be seeing them migrate up the Connecticut River to spawn.
They will then be considered true Connecticut River Atlantic Salmon.
This will represent the rare return of a subspecies that has been considered extinct.

Amcat and Gypsy

Dear Bowen,

This is another story about my beloved cat AMCAT. Do you remember the other story? You may not have read the other story about her, but if not it is fine. These stories are not in any particular order. This is a story about how Amcat was sick and what happened to her.

One day I noticed that Amcat was very quiet and did not come out to play as she usually did. She did not beg for breakfast. In fact, when I gave it to her, she did not eat. This was very unusual. She drank very little water. I knew something was wrong so I called the vet. He said I should bring her right in. It is quite serious when animals stop drinking. I took her to the vet so he could examine her. The only thing he detected in his exam was this; she had no bowel sounds. That can be a serious thing. So her vet took an abdominal x-ray to see what he could see. The x-ray showed a bowel obstruction. The vet asked if she ever had access to stuffing or soft cloth or some sort of object she might be able to lick or eat. I thought of how she liked to climb into an old couch I had. I knew she went in there at times because occasionally when I sat on the couch I could feel her moving around in there. I told the vet. He said he would have to keep her there in the animal hospital for a day or two while he tried to get her to pass the obstruction. He had medicine to accomplish that. If she could not pass it he would have to operate on her to get it out. That would be quite serious.

So I left Amcat there and I called a few times to get progress reports. The report was there was no progress. The obstruction was still there. A day passed and the vet called. He said according to new x-rays the obstruction had not moved. He was going to operate on Amcat as soon as he was finished with his office hours. That would be in late evening but he promised he would call as soon as the operation was finished so I would know how she tolerated the surgery. I was so worried I could not concentrate on the newspaper or a book or any of the things I liked to do in the evening. I could only think of poor little Amcat. You may remember Amcat was the 'runt' of her litter and never grew to be a big cat. She always had a kitten look to her although she did grow up. She was petite and sweet and I wanted her to come home safe and sound.

Finally the vet did call. He had not done the surgery. Just as he was about to take her in to the place where he did operations, he checked her one more time, and he heard faint bowel sounds. He gave her more of the medicine he had been giving her to help her pass the obstruction and waited. He examined her again. Another x-ray confirmed the obstruction had moved a little. He decided to wait longer before operating on her. Finally she passed the obstruction. She was going to be all right. He said he would call again in the morning unless something happened to her during the night. He got up during the night to check on her. You can see he was a very good vet who truly cared about his patients.

The next day the vet called and said the obstruction was clearly gone and she was probably OK, but sometimes cats who have this condition develop complications and he wanted to keep her there until she ate some food. He was at this time giving her intravenous fluids to keep her well hydrated. She would not eat. She sniffed the food and walked away. He called again later and said she was still not eating. If she would not start eating he would have to put a tube into her stomach to feed her, but he did not want to put her through that. He wanted more time. I said keep her until you think it is safe to bring her home. OK, he thought that was the best plan.

Finally he called and said she did not eat at all, and he thought maybe she was just too homesick. That is when a cat or person so misses home she cannot relax or do the normal things – like eat. He said he wanted me to bring Amcat home and see if she would eat if she felt safe in her own home. So I put out a big spread of her favorite foods; shrimp, fish, chicken, dry food, wet food, practically everything she had ever eaten.

By the way, before I picked Amcat up at the vet, I chopped that couch up in little pieces and threw the pieces out the second floor window so this could never happen again. The trash collector took it away to the dump.

Then I went to the vet and brought Amcat home. I showed her the food I had put out for her. She sniffed it and walked away. I was so upset. I followed her into the bedroom where she had found our dog. The dog's name was Gypsy. Amcat lay down near Gypsy so Gypsy could lick her. She licked Amcat all over, repeatedly, so much so that Amcat was dripping wet. She looked as if she had been swimming in a pond. The she went back to the food and ate until her little sides were puffing out she was so full. She had no further problems with the couch or with her appetite.

I told the vet what had transpired and he said she probably did not want to eat with that 'vet smell' on her. The dog washed it away. This is a true story about my Amcat and our companion Gypsy. They often washed each other before this event and after. They were good friends and they looked out for each other, as you can see from this little story. May you always have good friends and family to look out for you. May you always have someone who loves you to wash the vet smell off you so you can feel safe and hungry.

With much love,
Grandmom

Here is a picture of Gypsy and Amcat. They napped together every day, morning and evening. As you know from the story, they also bathed each other often.

Here is another photograph of those two good friends, Gypsy and Amcat. They loved to nap close together. This picture was taken in my apartment in Chicago.

UNCLE MATT AND YOUR GRANDPA

Dear Bowen,

This is a true story about your Uncle Matt and his Daddy, your Grandpa. When your Uncle Matt was about your age or perhaps a little older he had been hard at work playing with his toys and it was time to clean up. So Uncle Matt started putting his toys away. Since he was quite young I helped him put his toys in the toy box.

You probably remember that I am your Uncle Matt's Mommy. I am your Mommy's Mommy too. We were soon interrupted by your Grandpa who was frantically looking for his wallet. As you may know, wallets are the place where most people carry their driver's license and other cards. Those who have money usually carry that in their wallets too.

The word license actually means permission. It usually involves a government authority giving a citizen or visitor to our country permission to drive a car, operate a business, or in the case of your Mommy and me, permission to practice nursing. Many other persons need a professional license to work as well.

The driver's license is very important because it must be in possession of the driver of any car at all times. Any time there is an accident or any other reason for police to speak to the driver the first thing the officer will ask is to see the driver's license. So you can see why it was very important for your Grandpa to find his driver's license.

Well, it was not to be. Your Grandpa had to write to the Pennsylvania Department of Motor Vehicles for a replacement license. In Massachusetts they call it the Registry of Motor Vehicles which is only a small difference. States, like people, like to be different from others and make their mark as an "individual". Eventually Grandpa did get a new license. He had to pay money to get it, as the people who make the rules for the DMV do not like for people to lose their licenses. It was not his fault, however, as you will see. Grandpa also had to call his credit card company and cancel his credit cards, then he had to apply for a new card and that took some time. Eventually he bought a new wallet and put all his new cards in it.

Not long after, your Uncle Matt was very busy playing again. He was so busy he emptied his entire toy box. Later he needed to pick up his toys and put them back in the toy box. Once again I helped him. And guess what. There on the bottom of the toy box was one item with which Uncle Matt had not been playing. It was his Daddy's wallet, with his license and all the cards intact. The wallet had not been lost or stolen. Your Uncle Matt had simply picked it up and put it in the toy box when he was putting his toys away. No one noticed because it was small and fell all the way to the bottom. In the interim Uncle Matt had not totally emptied his toy box, so no one noticed the wallet was there.

Your Uncle Matt was happy and proud to have found his Daddy's wallet. He never thought about his having been the culprit who "lost" the wallet in the first place. His Daddy was happy the wallet had been found but he was disappointed it had not been found before he went to the expense and bother to get new cards and license. I was laughing because it was such a silly story. The lost wallet was in the toy box all that time and none of us knew it was there.

Did you know that play is a child's work? I think it is tragic that sometimes adults forget that and they forget how to play. May you have many happy hours of play, emptying your toy box and later putting your toys away. May you always remember how to play and may you always have someone cheering you on as you play and as you are busily putting your toys back in the box. No matter how old you are.

With much love,
Grandmom

Here is a photo of your Uncle Matt and his Dad, your Grandpa.
They arranged to have this
picture taken especially for your book.

ANCESTORS

Dear Bowen,

This is a true story about my ancestors, who are also your ancestors. You, however, have more ancestors than this short list. Your have ancestors from your Mommy's Daddy (your Grandpa), and from your Daddy's Mommy and Daddy too. So this is about one quarter of your ancestors, the only ones I know about. It is fun to know something about those people who have lived before us, given us life, and shown us by their example some of the things to do and some of the things we may want to avoid. You will discover which of these is which. You will decide the difference and the similarities and make your life choices accordingly.

Our ancestors came from Germany as mercenary soldiers to volunteer to fight in the war in 1776. That was called the War of Independence because the colonies became independent when the King of England tired of waging war here. It was more a matter of the King stopping the war (it was very expensive) rather than the colonists "winning" it. These ancestors of ours were farmers, but they had no land in Germany. They had to work for other people who did own land. So they decided to come and try to win some land. The leaders of the colonies had promised them if the war were "won" by the colonists here, land would be given to those who fought in what is now called the Revolutionary War. They did finally "win" the war and the new government honored its promise and gave land to the German (former) mercenaries, now settlers in this new land. They traveled many miles to pick the place where black walnut trees flourished. In Germany in the area of the Black Forest there were many black walnut trees so the settlers knew the land near those trees was good for farming. So they picked the area which is now known as the Pennsylvanish Deutch area of southeast Pennsylvania. You can see the words look like Pennsylvania Dutch and that is what the former German settlers were, and still are, called. But they are not and never were Dutch. The German word for German is Deutch and that is where the confusion enters the picture.

None of my grandparents spoke German as far as I know. My Mother's mother grew up on a farm and took a job in town (Reading) when she left the farm. She had some grammar school education but she did not, as far as I know, go to high school. She did, however, read the newspaper every day, every page, back to front. She was interested in what was going on in the world and she read what she could about it. As you know, I knew my Grandmom and I loved her dearly. She had three sisters and one brother. I knew Aunt Katie, Aunt Ruth, and Aunt Marie, but Uncle Percy died young, so I did not know him. I did not know my Great Grandmother either since she died before I was born. I did know my Great Grandfather, however. He lived with my Grandmom toward the end of his life, so I saw him often when we visited Grandmom.

My Mother's father is a mystery to all of us. I never met him as far as I know. My Mother did not know him, and Grandmom never spoke of him. I assume he was German since the majority of people in the area were of German descent. Of course if he were German or not does not change who we are.

My Father's father was not known to me either. My Dad grew up with him on the family farm, but my Grandpop died before I was born. I know little about him. I do know he was a strict disciplinarian and a hard worker. I know he was a farmer, and German. I know this from stories my Dad told me about his father.

My Father's mother was an interesting person. She had her own opinions and was strong in them, although women at that time were neither supposed to have nor express any opinions at all. She had several children. As was common at that time, some of her children did not live to adult age, so that must have been painful for her. She did not talk about that. When she retired she went to live with each of her children for a few months at a time. I remember her living with us for short periods of time and I always missed her when she went to live with another of her children. She too was German. Later, when her husband died, she sold her home and bought a big RV. She and a friend traveled all over the country seeing the sights and visiting friends and family.

My Mother did not finish High School, but she was smart and loved words. She was an avid reader and she was a good friend to those who grew up with her in her neighborhood. She had a wonderful sense of humor and she had a great laugh. She was close to your Mommy and your Uncle Matt and she took great pride in them and their accomplishments. She always wanted to be a nurse. She referred to the day I was graduated from nursing school as the best day of her life. She did not have many of the opportunities I have had.

I may have been the first woman of my family to be graduated from high school. I am certain I was the first to be graduated from college. My brother was graduated from college, as was my Dad. In the 1950s, women were not expected to attend nor graduate from college, unless they were to be teachers. I preferred nursing, but at that time student nurses studied at a school affiliated with a hospital and earned a diploma, but not an academic degree. Some years after being graduated from nursing school, I was able to finish my college degree. Your Mommy and Uncle Matt came to the graduation. Ask if they remember.

Each generation has had more opportunities and a broader view of life than the ones before. You will have a much broader understanding of life than your ancestors. They have paved a path for you to tread. There are many other stories about your ancestors. I know a few of them, and I will share more of them with you at a later time. I do know that your ancestors are proud of you and truly love you. And of course you know that your Grandmom loves you and loves sharing stories with you.

With much love,
Grandmom

This picture shows a farm house amidst farmland in the Black Forest.
Our ancestors probably came from this region.
Photosearch image used here with permission.

This is a five generation picture. The youngest in the picture is your cousin Ken.
He was sound asleep for the occasion. Your great great grandmother Lachman is holding him.
Seated next to her is her mother, your great great great grandmother Rhodes.
Standing is your great grandfather Lachman, and next to him is your Uncle Tav.

This is a picture of your great great Grandmom and her eldest son, Augustus Clark. She was my beloved Grandmom, who danced with me in my dream. He was known as "Bud". His sister, my Mother, was called "Sis".

This is a family photo from early in the last century. Standing at left is my Aunt Ruth, who let me play in the woods. Next to her is Aunt Katie, the oldest child. Standing on the right is my Grandmom (Florence). Sitting in the middle is the youngest, Aunt Marie. Neither sitting nor standing is Uncle Percy.

This is a picture of Aunt Ruth, holding your Uncle Matt when he was just a wee one. Aunt Ruth had no children of her own, but she was an Aunt to many children, some who were related to her and many who were not.

This is a picture of your Grandmom when she was about a year old. At that time there was no color photography. Rather, people had black and white photographs taken. Later the pictures were taken to an artist who added the color.

MISS MAGNOLIA BLOSSOM

Dear Bowen,

This is a story about Maggie. You know her well. She often comes with me when I come to visit you at your house. On some occasions she stays at your house when I need to go to a place where dogs are not allowed. This is rare, but it does happen occasionally. Maggie likes you, and she likes being at your house. I know that because she whines when she gets close to your house. That means she knows where she is going and she is eager to get there as soon as possible.

Maggie has a story of her own. In July, 2002, when she was only three or four months old, Maggie was hit by a car and then was taken to a pound (that's a shelter) in Tennessee. There are no vets available at the pound. No one knows where she was before that. The people at the pound were not able to find anyone who knew her or claimed to own her. Personally, I do not think of myself as owning the animals who share my home. They are my companions, not my property.

A wonderful woman saw Maggie in the shelter and knew she needed to be seen by a vet. She paid to take Maggie out of the pound, then took her to a vet who x-rayed her and found she had a broken pelvis and a broken leg. She also had a torn anterior crusciate ligament. She needed surgery, but who would pay for it? Maggie had no money and no one to take care of her. Maggie was left at the vet's office to get the treatment she needed. If Maggie were a recognizable breed the breed rescue organization would have paid for her surgery. The woman who rescued her worked with a German Shepherd rescue organization. Alas, Maggie looked nothing like a German Shepherd. The vet said he would operate on her regardless. He fixed Maggie's leg and people who saw her on the internet donated money to pay the vet bill. Maggie spent a few days at the hospital after the surgery. The splint on her leg was nearly as big as she was. She was not yet full grown, and she weighed about 32 pounds.

Maggie's new best friend asked a woman she knew, named Karen, to be a foster mom for Maggie. Karen agreed, although she had many other dogs. Maggie quickly adjusted to Karen's house. She liked the food and she liked having other dogs to play with, although she could not play much while the splint was on her leg. She did not want to walk on her splinted leg so Karen carried her. I have read that it is possible to judge the values of a society by noting how the people care for children, elderly, and animals. Karen would pass with flying colors! If we were all like her, this world would be like paradise. Maggie learned from Karen and Ed that people can be kind, compassionate, and gentle with dogs. Their care gave Maggie a good foundation to be the dog she is now; social, playful, protective. But I digress.

After the splint came off her leg Maggie had to swim every day so her leg would gain strength. Ed and Karen took Maggie into their pool to strengthen her leg after weeks in a cast. Although she hated the pool, she did swim every day, and it did make her leg stronger. Eventually her leg was better and the swimming was over. She began to play and run just like all the other dogs. By that time she weighed about 40 pounds. Karen wanted to find a good forever home for Maggie (who was called Loretta then). Someone from Connecticut (me) contacted Karen about wanting to adopt Maggie. After a fairly long process which was intended to be sure Maggie had a good home, she was ready for her trip to Connecticut, her new home, and her forever family. You are a part of that family, Bowen, and Maggie is fortunate to have a boy who likes to play but knows how to play without hurting dogs. You, Bowen, are that little boy. You have learned so much in the few years since you were born.

Maggie came to Connecticut just before Christmas in 2002. She was about a year old at the time. She came with a collar, a leash, and a new toy. She was lonely when she first came. She missed Skylar, her best doggie friend at Karen's house, and she missed Ed and Karen most of all. She not only had to get used to a totally different house and yard, she had to get used to new people as well. I could tell she was not comfortable here because she crawled under the holiday tree and was very reluctant to come out. I let her stay there but I sat on the floor, close to her so she would know I cared about her, and I would not hurt her. She had to get used to two cats who set about teaching her that she was well below them in the hierarchy, without question. She still defers to cats when they sit in front of her water bowl. She waits for them to move before getting her drink. She has become very close to one of the cats here now, but that is a story for another day. She has doggie friends here. Her best friend in the neighborhood is Jake, who lives across the street. They like to run in the woods and on the beach. She likes Ozzie, who runs with her on your beaches, both one and two. There are a few other dogs she likes lots. Some include Snoopy, Buddy, Trey, and Ringo. They are nice to her, and never make fun of her southern accent. I think she still would like to run with Skylar, but it is a far commute. Perhaps some day we will take a trip to Tennessee.

Maggie had to get used to lots of snow. She had seen snow in Tennessee, but Connecticut storms usually drop more snow on the ground. We recently had a fairly good storm here, with a total of about ten inches of snow over a few days. She likes to run in the snow as well as roll on her back in the snow. She makes me laugh when she does that. Maybe she does it partly to entertain me. She had to learn to sit and wait when a door opened so she would not knock children (nor old ladies) over when she runs out the door. She had to learn not to get up on furniture. Many in the family do not mind if she would get on the furniture, but some would have a problem with it. So in order to let Maggie come with me more often, she has to stay off all furniture. To teach her that, I pushed her off the couch as gently as I could, and said down. I did it only twice, and she never got up on the furniture again. I sat on the floor with her so she would know she was loved, although she was not to get up on the couch. She rarely barks, but she growls if she is around someone she does not trust. That happened a few times, and I find if Maggie does not trust a person, neither do I.

Here is one more little detail about Maggie's story. I wanted to honor Maggie's history of being from the south, which is where Tennessee is located. So I thought Miss Magnolia Blossom would be a good name for her. She responds to that as well as to "Maggie". She came to live here not long after her predecessor Puppy died. I had some thoughts that perhaps I was looking for another dog too soon. I did not want Puppy to think he could be easily replaced. He was a very good dog and I loved him lots. He had cancer and no one had any idea until his abdominal tumor began to bleed. His vet knew there was something very wrong, but did not know exactly what that was. Puppy died the same day we discovered he was sick; too sick to recover from that illness. I had him cremated so he would not be left alone somewhere. When pets are cremated the vet returns the ashes to the family with whom they lived. Puppy's ashes came in a lovely tin with magnolia blossoms all over it. I knew then that it was OK with Puppy for Maggie to come live with us, and he did not feel badly that I chose to get another dog. Maggie is like Puppy in many ways, but is very different in many ways too. She is a very good dog, a credit to her foster family, a smart little girl, in many ways my best friend.

May you always have a true companion as loyal and loving as your Ozzie and my precious Maggie.

With much love,
Grandmom

Here is a close up picture of Maggie, taken in a nearby park.
You may be able to notice a little grey on her muzzle.
Since that picture was taken, she has grown a little more grey on her face and around her eyes. As you no doubt know, she is truly beautiful to me.

Your Mommy and Daddy

Dear Bowen,

Several years ago, before your parents wed, they went on a Mountain Workshop adventure together. Daddy works for Mountain Workshop helping children learn about conservation, nature, orienteering in the woods, and other outdoor skills. On one occasion he was about to take a group of children to learn to climb, then rappel off a cliff. He invited your Mommy to come along, and she eagerly accepted. She knew he would be good with children, according to the way he talked about them. She wanted to see him in action with kids.

First your Daddy told the children what they had to do to rappel safely. When he was certain they understood what he was saying, he told them to "go". One by one the children rappelled off the cliff, using the ropes and the instructions he had painstakingly given them. All of the kids were able to put the lesson into practice except one. From the top of the cliff the task looked a little different from the same lesson given on level ground. Your Daddy was on the bottom, telling the kids they were doing great, correcting them if they forgot part of the lesson, encouraging them.

Your Mommy was on the top, making sure they were holding the ropes properly, reminding them to look up, not down. She also encouraged them, telling them they were doing great, which in fact they were doing. Remember, this was their first time rappelling. One of the children was almost ready to move off the cliff and he froze. He was suddenly very frightened, and told your Mommy he could not do it. She talked him into trying it, knowing if he did not try, it would make him feel less competent to do all of the things he needed to do, indoors and out. She told him he needed to look into her face, and not look down. He finally agreed to do that. She reminded him to look at her if he started to look away. She kept telling him he was almost there, and indeed eventually he was there! The other children had already finished the exercise, and when that last child's feet contacted the ground a great cheer rose from the children on the ground. He did it!

One of the things your Daddy always did when he worked with a group of children was to remind them to appreciate what they had each day they went camping or doing outdoor exercises. The children would sit in a circle and take turns saying what they appreciated about that day. They boy who overcame his fear said he appreciated your Mommy for helping him get over his fear so he could rappel. He then said he felt as if he could now do anything, no matter how frightened he might feel. What a gift this child now has, given by the love your mommy and daddy have for all children, especially those who are frightened or sick. Remember, this story is true, although it happened before you were born.

Your Mommy went back to school a few years before you were born. She became a nurse. During her time of practice in the hospital she worked in the Intensive Care Unit at Yale. Of all the places to work in a hospital, that is one of the hardest, most stressful, important jobs in the world. While she was there as a student, they told her there would be two openings at the hospital, both in intensive care. One in the general ICU, the other in the Pediatric ICU. She applied for both jobs as they requested, and she was offered both. She chose to work with the children in the PICU. She has worked there ever since. It is an intense, challenging job, and she is exhausted by it, but she is also very good at it. She plans to continue working there for some time. Recently she also went back to school, with the goal of becoming a Family Nurse Practitioner. She will work hard at that job too, but she will not have to work night shift. That is a good thing.

This story is to tell you about one of the things which drew your parents together. Their love of children. Of all the children they have worked with, of all the children they have helped, of all the children they have come to care about, YOU and your little brother are the most important of all. They love you so much, and they try so hard to take the best care of you that they possibly can.

Someday you will have to choose a career. You might want to do something to help children too. You might want to do some other kind of work. You love trains; maybe you will help build them, or design trains which run quickly and safely. You also like cars. You like reading and numbers. There are many kinds of work you can do. You are very smart, so you will be able to do whatever you choose to do. You will not be limited by your brain nor your strong little body. Maybe you will be a teacher, or an athlete.

Whatever you choose to do, you can be sure you will have the full, total support of your Mommy and Daddy, who love you very much. As for me, I will support you will all my strength, no matter what. The rest of your family will too.

With much love,
Grandmom

This picture was taken on the day your Mommy and Daddy worked together to help the children learn rock climbing and rappelling.

Here is a picture of your Mommy and Daddy dancing at a wedding reception. They dance well together, and they work well together too. Most importantly, they parent well together.

GRANDMOM'S BOOK PROJECT

Dear Bowen,

Today I took a step into the future. We all have some plan for our future. Some plans concern our education, our career, our family, or other major concerns of our lives.

As you know, I started writing stories for you for your first birthday present. I have written several stories thus far, and I plan to write more. I have a list of stories which I have thought might interest you, and I continue to write them as I have time. Now that I am truly retired, I have more time and a strong interest in writing for you. I have also written some stories for your little brother August, and he will have a book too. Many of the stories are similar or even nearly the same as stories I have written for you. Others are specifically for him. This is so you will each have your own book to read as you get older and learn more about letters, words, and life.

I have been proud of you Bowen, as I see you recognize letters and many words. You even understood a little joke I told recently about a dog whose name is god (dog spelled backwards). As you get older the stories I have written may have more appeal to you. Many are about our family and some are about your Mommy and your Uncle Matt. As you may remember, your Mommy and your Uncle Matt are my children, and so I have included some stories about them when they were little children.

One of the reasons I have had the idea to write stories is my love for my own Grandmom. She returned to the spirit world many years ago. I have often thought to ask her questions about her life as a young girl, her thoughts about the newspaper which she read every day. I want to ask her so many questions now that I am grown, but she is gone and cannot answer me. So as I was thinking about this, and when your Mommy asked me to tell her of a family gathering about which she had only a vague memory, I decided to write some stories so you will know what went on in our family and in the world when you were a little boy, and even earlier, before you were born.

The point of this letter is to tell you that I have decided to have these stories published in the form of a book. I will give you the book when it is published, and I will sign it for you. August will have his book too. The most important thing for you to remember about this project, Bowen, is that it is a labor of love. It is meant to tell you with each page, with each word, how dearly you are loved.

May you read the words and feel the strong bond which we are forming each day we spend together.

With much love,
Grandmom

Here is a picture of you and your Grandmom.
How I love that little smile, those bright blue eyes, your laugh.
Most of all I love when you run to the door when I come and you call out "Grandmom!"
Thank you for all those beautiful days…

CPSIA information can be obtained
at www.ICGtesting.com
Printed in the USA
270353LV00002B